In Good Company

With all
good wishes
Yours ever
George Baxendale.

will love & thanks to you
& Stanley
Jean N. Mayland.

Love from Lesley Macdonald

To a dear sister in grace!
With love from Margaret

With since good
wishes..... we will
get there!
Nell Brownlow

Elizabeth Wardlaw

In Good Company
Women in the Ministry

Lesley Orr Macdonald (ed)

WILD GOOSE PUBLICATIONS

Copyright © 1999 Lesley Orr Macdonald and the contributors

First published 1999 by
Wild Goose Publications
Unit 16, Six Harmony Row, Glasgow G51 3BA

Wild Goose Publications is the publishing division of the
Iona Community. Scottish Charity No. SCO03794.
Limited Company Reg. No. SCO96243.

ISBN 1 901557 15 4

Cover illustration: Elizabeth Howe memorial window © Mari Girling.
Reproduced with permission from Jeremy Howe
and St Anne's College, Oxford.
Cover design: Gillian Park

A catalogue record for this book is available
from the British Library.

Distributed in Australia and New Zealand by Willow Connection Pty Ltd,
Unit 7A, 3-9 Kenneth Road, Manly Vale, NSW 2093, Australia.

Permission to reproduce any part of this work in Australia
or New Zealand should be sought from Willow Connection.

Printed by Bell & Bain, Thornliebank, Glasgow

Contents

Contributors

Joanna Anderson *Anglican priest*

Georgina Baxendale *Church of Scotland minister*

Helen Blackburn *Advocate for the ordination of Catholic women priests*

Lesley Carroll *Presbyterian minister*

Margaret Forrester *Church of Scotland minister*

Alison Fuller *Scottish Episcopal priest*

Ruth Harvey *Director of the Ecumenical Spirituality Project for Churches Together in Britain and Ireland*

Viv Lassetter *Baptist minister*

Kate McIlhagga *United Reformed Church minister*

Jean Mayland *Anglican priest*

Lesley Orr Macdonald *Action for Churches Together in Scotland*

Katharine Poulton *Church of Ireland priest*

Elizabeth Wardlaw *United Free Church minister*

1 Introduction

Lesley Orr Macdonald

On Wednesday 20 May, 1998, a tall and distinguished senior minister of the Church of Scotland addressed the General Assembly; not from the 'playpen' at the front of the hall, but from under the gallery at the back:

> *Moderator, I choose to speak from here, because this is where I stood 35 years ago, very frightened, facing an entirely male Assembly whom I had to persuade to examine what I believed to be my call from God to the Ministry of Word and Sacrament. How vastly different the Assembly is today!*

Mary Levison (or Lusk, as she was in 1963) is encountered in several places, on many of the paths walked by the contributors to this book. She is, truly, a pioneer among women seeking the right to have their vocation to Christian ordained ministry tested and affirmed. Her gifts and her grace, her courage and her persistence have inspired the endeavours of many other women. But she has also been a companion – both to those who know her personally, and to those who realised that they did not have to travel alone on journeys which could be tedious and treacherous, with many obstacles and obstructions. Mary Levison tells her own story in her own book, *Wrestling with the Church*. This present book, *In Good Company*, maps out the paths made by twelve other women, from Scotland, England and Ireland, whose lives have been shaped by their experiences of being called to minister in the church and in the world.

The ministry of women has been a subject of ecclesiastical deliberation and debate throughout the history of the Christian church. Male clerics and theologians – Catholic, Protestant, Orthodox – have taken it upon themselves to pontificate in Synods, Councils and Assemblies about the nature, position and divinely

Huge advances have been made. One has only to look around this Assembly – not only at the numbers of women who are Commissioners, but also three women 'up there' [the 'playpen'] in positions of authority. And in today's Sederunt, two previous items of business led by women. There is now no discrimination in the law of the Church in any offices of ministry; and I exult as much in the admission of men to the diaconate as I do in women to the ministry (or nearly as much!). This has been achieved without a split, or I think any danger of a split, in the Kirk. A gradual development, slow it may seem to some, but sure. The Church has truly been reformed, is truly being reformed in this respect.

Truly, indeed, the church has changed. Women, in most Protestant denominations, can no longer be excluded from ministry simply because they are women. But is that enough? If we simply 'add women and stir', what difference, if any, does that make to the bread which is the Body of Christ alive in the world? If female ordained ministers are just incorporated into an old, stale recipe, is the church any fresher or more nourishing?

Women who have walked through the door have often had to live with hard questions; with stereotypes and assumptions; with personal and practical challenges which sometimes seem to call into question their right to follow their call, by treating female ministers as a 'problem' for the church. Are they subjected to tokenism, or co-option into the old boys club? Do they suffer discrimination and trivialisation? Are they open to abuse and isolation? Is there a 'stained glass ceiling'? Have they bought into an institution obsessed with power, rank and position?

And what about the women who still stand at the door and knock (or batter very hard, but with, apparently, no response)? What kind of church do they want to serve?

Women in ordained ministry have in some senses become 'normal'. But, paradoxically, they remain both newsworthy and controversial, and also invisible or silenced. While I write this introduction, I have been aware of different stories and images:

• A Church of England report indicates widespread sexual,

physical and emotional harassment of women priests by their colleagues and within church structures.

- A Church of Scotland conference about 'Ministry in the new Millennium' has no female speakers or contributors.

- The Vatican has banned any discussion or debate about the theology or possibility of women in the priesthood.

- A 'rebel' Irish bishop plans to 'ordain' a nun to the priesthood. She will serve a worshipping community in Co. Antrim.

- A young single woman minister is seeking to take the Church of Scotland before an industrial tribunal, claiming that she was unfairly forced to resign after being wrongly accused of sexual immorality. She maintains that, instead, she was the victim of a sexual assault.

- Ordained women can be the stuff of situation comedy or TV advertising (where the impact depends on the juxtaposition of stereotyped vicars with the unexpectedly jolly, straight-talking Vicar of Dibley; or the glamorous woman, rushing to get ready for a wedding, who turns out to be officiating).

The paradigm shift which has made it possible for women to be ordained has also challenged traditional understandings of church and God; of community and ministry. The adland female priest, whose uncomfortable and potentially embarrassing infection almost makes her late for the wedding, wears the traditional dog-collar and cassock, along with her mini-skirt and high heels. But that garb can (and has often been used to) symbolise the hierarchical authority, the professionalism, the 'set-apartness' of ordained ministry.

Attitudes towards appropriate attire can reveal a lot about the theology and practice of ministry. I remember listening to a fascinating debate among ordained women in Ireland. Some believed that it was essential for them to be seen in the distinctive clothes of their profession – especially in a society so dominated by men and religion! They argued that it was vital to confront people with the reality that women could, and should, inhabit the ministry, and therefore command the respect and authority accorded to those who hold church office. Others maintained that ordination was not a calling to power or position; nor was their calling any more significant or noteworthy than the vocation of other Christians. They described ministry as with, not to, the people, and wanted to identify themselves with the folk in the community they served, rather than with a particular professional caste. They sought to challenge the complacency and conservatism of the establishment, and did not object to the apparent invisibility of not being immediately identified as a 'minister'. For some women, on both sides of this discussion, gender was a key factor in their self-understanding and experience of what it means to be ordained. For others, it was less important. And, of course, neither the discussion nor the lived reality is quite so black and white. Labels like 'radical' or 'conservative'; 'feminist' or 'traditional' can be dog-collars too: badges of identity, or barriers which prevent communication and can choke out life.

What does it mean to minister faithfully and with integrity? In recent years, and in the light of their traditional exclusion from ordination, women who believe they have a vocation to ministry have responded in different ways. These have, to some extent, been shaped by the positions of the traditions to which they belong. The responses have also been influenced by personal, theological and cultural factors.

Some women, believing that the institutional church is irredeemably patriarchal, hurtful and decadent – or simply that it has no meaning for their life of spirit and action – have left. For some this has been a deeply painful and distressing departure. For others it has been a natural and positive process. There are many who (intentionally or otherwise) are now building or reaching out to new communities of faith and purpose.

Other women, perceiving the call of God, have simply asked for the chance to test that call; to prepare for and conduct an ordained ministry within the church to which they belong. Of course, that path is not at all simple, as those who have travelled along it have testified. But there are ordained women, or those who seek ordination, who have no strong urge to challenge or change the structures, institutions, practices and habits of their church – even though they may be well aware that these are far from perfect! Once the doors have been opened, they seek only a fair opportunity to exercise their personal ministry, according to the gifts and possibilities God has granted them.

And other women are committed, not to separation or integration, but to the transformation of the church. In this process, they live with the tension between what is and what might be. They belong, yet they struggle with the language, the theologies, the traditions and the prejudices by which Christian churches have demeaned, patronised, limited and excluded not only women, but countless human beings created in the image and intention of God. Their journey is a complicated one – sometimes moving towards the centres of ecclesiastical power but more often finding themselves (by choice or necessity) on the rough edges of the church's efforts to be a 'holy city', where the roads are rutted or unpaved; where the paths and the signposts stop; where things get messy and scary.

The women who share their stories in this book have all (so far) chosen not to separate themselves from the church. What does it mean to minister with faith and integrity? For each of the contributors, the answer to that question includes a decision to remain as part of the church. And so this book is about women in the Christian church. When she spoke at the 1998 General Assembly, Mary Levison addressed her closing words to those who still do not accept that God calls women into ministry:

> *To such I would say just one thing: Stand first at the foot of the Cross, where you will find your companions are women (the men, according to Scripture, having all turned and fled). Then stand at the empty tomb on Easter morning, and again according to Scripture, you will hear the risen Christ address Mary Magdalene and say to her, 'Go to my brothers and tell them – tell them I am about to ascend to my Father.' There is here a clear Apostolic Succession – women witnessing to the death and resurrection of Christ. What more will it take to persuade you?*[5]

The fact that we are living in the first generation in which significant numbers of women are able to exercise that apostolic commission gives us the right to ask: Does it make any difference? But it does not mean that we can assume the existence of particular qualities, practices, attitudes or insights which can be defined as 'women's ministry'. I am very suspicious of attempts to categorise or determine the glorious, diverse complexity of human experience and relationship. There is no such thing as 'Woman' whose reality can be named, controlled and confined. Individual women, like men, are different in their circumstances, upbringing, aptitudes, beliefs and motivations. It is our human right, and our joy, to be what we can be; what we choose to be.

Nevertheless, only the foolish or the naive would ignore the weight of tradition, theologies, structures and cultures which have been used to exclude and limit women. Churches are patriarchal institutions, in which power has too often been assumed – and exercised – to dominate, not to enable. They have evolved male-defined patterns of leadership, authority, control. The experience of women within churches cannot but be shaped, to some extent, by that historical reality which manifests itself in a variety of ways within different denominations. So it is legitimate to ask about the similarities, the connections, the common features (as well as the unique aspects) linking the journeys of women who have struggled for, or achieved, the right to ordination.

But this book is not a comparative study of the situation in different denominations (although, in Chapter 2, Jean Mayland presents a helpful overview of developments within churches of the British Isles). It is not a theoretical analysis of female ordination, or of new paradigms for church and ministry, or a theological textbook. It is not a comprehensive or representative survey of women priests and ministers. The contributors are Scottish, Irish and English. They belong to Presbyterian, United Reformed, Anglican, Baptist and Roman Catholic traditions; there are no voices from Wales, or from the Congregational, Methodist, Salvation Army, Society of Friends, Pentecostal or black-led churches. Of course there are women who minister in all of these contexts – and others

– and there should be many spaces and places for their testimony. This is simply a story book, with pictures. The images include paths and pilgrimages; looms and tapestries; cairns and angels; sisters and mothers and hags; doors and rocks. There are snapshots and group portraits, captured in flickering candlelight or in the glare of publicity. The colours are vibrant and muted, bold and muddy.

Keeping company . . .

Each story is unique and personal. But the women do not travel alone. They are surrounded by parents, partners, children and friends; by mentors and heroines; by opponents and by incredibly diverse communities of people; by clouds of biblical and historical witnesses, and by the supporting love of God.

What does it mean to minister with faith and integrity? For each person here, there are no neat, clean, solitary answers, worked out in advance. Each one has to take account of the complicated, compromising, agonising, revitalising business of connection and engagement with real life – her own and others'.

I once spoke to a woman who had suffered long years of physical abuse, emotional torture and personal degradation at the hands of her husband, who was a minister. She felt bitter, betrayed and abandoned by the church, and she was particularly cynical about the motives and actions of ordained ministers. But when she moved to a new neighbourhood, she encountered the local minister:

> *She came to me when I was at my lowest ebb, depressed and angry, and with my self-esteem destroyed. She didn't talk at me, or tell me I should be coming to church. She didn't try to solve my problems for me. She simply came, and listened, and believed me and did not judge me. She was present when I needed her, she kept me company when I felt really alone. She stuck with me and didn't flinch from my gaping wounds, but she wasn't a 'voyeur' either – other people saw me only as villain or victim. That woman was my companion through the wilderness. She helped restore my faith in my whole self, and in other people, and in God.*

The stories here are stories about keeping company: they are stories of women who exercise a ministry of presence, and who in turn are served by those who keep company with them on their journey.

. . . with those who are different

Lesley Carroll, writing in the midst of a community which for so long has been defined by difference, believes that separating ourselves from those with whom we don't agree is a failed pattern for the church, as it is for the wider community. She says here:

> *We have to learn to live together, with all our differences . . . God didn't choose to push us away and write us off because we were different. God chose our company. God chose the price of keeping company with those who were different.*

In their different ways and situations, Jean, and Elizabeth, and Margaret, Kate, and Katherine, and Georgina, Alison, and Joanna, and Viv, Lesley, Helen and Ruth have all chosen to keep company with those who are different.

Jean Mayland has been at the forefront, in England and at global level, of the struggle for ordination to priesthood of women in the Anglican Communion. She tells of the frustrations, the hurts and the joys of that 'Pilgrimage to Priesthood'. At the very moment of triumph, in a televised interview, she turned to one of the leading opponents: 'I put my hand on his hand, and said that we needed him – "Please don't go, stay with us, we need you." '

Elizabeth Wardlaw left the Church of Scotland because it would not, at that time, recognise her call, and was one of the first Scottish women to serve a congregation when she went to Hermitage United Free Church in Leith. She encountered many who saw her as 'different' – at theological college, in her pastoral duties, and when she spoke out in support of women's ordination. Over forty years of ministry, she has kept company with others, through her church, ecumenical and political involvement, to share her vision of Leith as an inclusive, welcoming community 'which shines with the light of God upon its life'.

Margaret Forrester, as a gifted young woman in the Church of Scotland, was set along the wrong paths for her service, until she was enabled to obey the call to ministry of Word and Sacrament. At the beginning of her parish ministry, she was told that they had only chosen her because they were forced to scrape the bottom of the barrel! Eighteen years of keeping committed and adventurous company with that congregation and community has been an experience of mutual learning, grace, forgiveness and generosity.

Kate McIlhagga's life bears witness to the fruits of discernment and preparation; of wisdom and vulnerability; of patience and passion. In so many ministries – with young people, students, the bereaved, in new housing schemes, in an ecumenical parish, in hospital and RAF chaplaincies, and now in her 'secret kingdom' of Northumbria – Kate has lived and worked on the exposed borderlands between happiness and sorrow, hope and despair.

As one of the first women to be priests in the Church of Ireland, *Katharine Poulton* has, with quiet resolution, worked to make 'difference' normal, acceptable, creative. To enable those she serves to know the loving presence of God. She tells the story of one disturbing encounter, on the road to lead worship in a Roman Catholic church in Portadown, with members of her congregation who could not accept her decision to do this. But others accompanied her and supported cross-community initiatives. Keeping company with those who are different has a high cost, as folk in the north of Ireland know too well.

Georgina Baxendale is in the throes of a lifelong adolescent crisis: she doesn't know whether she loves or hates her mother church! She struggles with the tendency to count power, importance, bigness and 'success' as valuable, when she knows that what really matters is to be faithful. Still, she puts up with the relationship – it may be for life, but perhaps there is a get-out clause . . .

For *Alison Fuller*, on the journey towards women's ordination in the Scottish Episcopal Church, the sense of isolation, of hearing her solo woman's voice amongst all the male ordinands, has been counteracted by the companionship and solidarity of those women (and some men) who choose to travel together in the Movement for Whole Ministry. For them, and for all who share their stories here, it is true that there are no 'women' in abstract: there are always only embodied, thinking, feeling, touching, living human beings.

To be an explorer of new territory can be exciting, but sometimes lonely. *Joanna Anderson* has created many paths where none have been before. In Scunthorpe, on Iona, in rural Norfolk, in family life and ecumenical engagement she has struggled to seek new ways to touch the hearts of all.

How many Baptist ministers are surrounded by a glorious company of women which includes a dynasty of Irish Catholic story-telling aunts? *Viv Lassetter's* encounters with difference have taken her on a journey into a 'singing church', and beyond, at the behest of God, to places of risk and passion and breadth of vision. To a growing sense of possibility, affirmation and solidarity as a woman of faith.

As a Presbyterian woman in Northern Ireland, exposed to the barbs of exclusion, scorn and downright rudeness from men of her own tradition, *Lesley Carroll* asks profound questions at the heart of our human efforts to be a faithful church. In a world of suspicion and hatred, separation and indifference, desolation and destruction, what alternative models does the church offer for dealing with difference? For her, some of the answers have been discovered in community with people who inhabit the fringes of society. In keeping company with them, she has met and been challenged by Jesus Christ.

Women of the Roman Catholic Church cannot become priests. They are not even supposed to think, or read, about the possibility. To openly express a vocation, and to campaign for it to be recognised, is to display difference – with pride: which is how *Helen Blackburn* wears her purple ribbon as part of the Catholic Women's Ordination Organisation. Yet she has a deep love and loyalty for her church. To keep such company, in a time of waiting and longing, is difficult; to be the focus for so much fear can be heartbreaking. But it brings its own opportunities to reflect about the shape of a church which truly believes in a priesthood of all believers.

Ruth Harvey's life is woven from a pattern of threads: community, church, conviction, relationships. The many-coloured cloth of her ministry is created out of collaboration, hard work, sharing, struggling together, listening, growing. It is surely a warm and companionable garment – if a wee bit frayed around the edges! Ruth has chosen not 'the' ministry of Word and Sacrament but a lay ministry of encounter, which includes challenge as well as acceptance; questioning as part of mutual connections. For her, 'friendship is not about being a "yes-woman" but about plain speaking and unconditional love. I would hope that in a model of ministry based on friendship, this kind of love and plain speaking could be at the core.'

Practical theologian James Newton Poling has written:

> *Reflection begins with the presence of difference and otherness in experience. Difference provokes thought. When persons or communities become aware of some desire that contrasts with identity, the potential contradiction requires reflection. Self-conscious lived experience is filled with the tension of similarity and difference, and identity becomes stronger as these tensions are faced and worked through. This means that otherness must be preserved as a window into the depths of ultimate reality. Without difference and contrast, there can be no self-conscious experience.*[5]

Reflection on the encounter with difference can lead to awareness of the need for, and possibility of, change. It is a source of growth, grace, transformation. This, I believe, has been true for each of the women in this story book. It can also be true for the church, as it begins to keep company with the difference embodied in the ministry of women. We have reached the end of the Ecumenical Decade of Churches in Solidarity with Women (1988–98). Reflecting on the implications of the Decade, Irja Askola, a Finnish Lutheran pastor and poet, suggests that the deep longing of so many women for a spiritual community of justice, care and sanctuary challenges the very self-understanding of the church:

We remember the Canaanite woman as one of our foremothers (Matt 15:21–28). It was not easy for her. She had her point, her reason to be concerned. And yet how hard it was for her to be heard, to be understood, to be taken seriously. Jesus had other priorities and good theological arguments; his loyalty to tradition and to his own mandate gave him a right to silence her, to leave her alone in her pain, to wish he had never met her on his journey. But she does not leave him alone; all her emotions and all her intellect are face to face with his embarrassment and his doctrinal logic. A dialogue: both of these two are learning something. Did she know before how strong she was, that she could be the equal, in an argument, of a man she did not even know, and with whom she was not supposed to speak? Had he ever experienced a challenge from a woman; had he known before how it feels to change one's own mind. God in Jesus encounters a woman like many of us, who shares her experience of harsh treatment on the road. Somewhere hidden in our hearts lives hope, a foretaste of joy – that what happened one day to Jesus might happen to others as well, one day . . .[6]

I thank this company of twelve apostles for telling their stories; for sharing in dialogue; for being present in the lives of so many people; and for ministering to the transforming power of a loving God.

Notes and References

1. See especially Elisabeth Schussler Fiorenza, *In Memory of Her: A Feminist Theological Reconstruction of Christian Origins.* London, SCM, 1983.

2. From Martin Luther's commentary on Genesis 3:16

3. See Lesley Orr Macdonald, *A Unique and Glorious Mission: Women and Presbyterianism in Scotland, c1830–1930.* Edinburgh, John Donald, 1999.

4. Proceedings and Debates of the General Assembly of the United Free Church of Scotland, 1926, p215

5. James Newton Poling, *The Abuse of Power: A Theological Problem.* Nashville, Abingdon Press (1991) p187

6. Irja Askola (Conference of European Churches), speech in Rome, March 1998.

2　*Pilgrimage to Priesthood and Beyond*

Jean Mayland

At last,
standing in the robes of the church.
'We are the body of Christ,' I say.
(So God created humanity in his image)

At last,
standing at the altar of the church,
'Take, eat, this is my body,' I say.
(In the image of God he created them)

At last,
I break the bread
and hold the two halves.
(Male and female he created them)
Humanity made whole in the body of Christ.

(By a woman priest ordained in Durham)

The World Council of Churches and women

In 1975 I attended the Fifth Assembly of the World Council of Churches in Nairobi. I had been involved in ecumenism at the local level, but this was my first experience on the world stage. The theme of the Assembly was 'Jesus Christ Frees and Unites'. The theme song of the Assembly had the refrain: 'Break down the walls that separate us and unite us in a single body.' One of the barriers which the Assembly sought to break down was that between men and women. It was the Nairobi Assembly that received the report of the Berlin Conference on Sexism in the 1970s and went on to set up the Study Programme on the Community of Women and Men in the Church. The importance of this programme is still reflected in the *raison d'être* of my job at the Council of Churches for Britain and Ireland (now Churches Together in Britain and Ireland), which gives me the title: 'Associate Secretary for the Community of Women and Men in the Church'.

In setting up this Study Programme the WCC was taking a step forward and attempting to challenge the churches more strongly, but it was also acting in a way that was consistent with its actions from the beginning. As Susannah Herzel points out in the foreword to her book *A Voice for Women*:

> *Since the 1940s there has been working within the World Council of Churches an intentional fellowship of men and women committed to restoring that mutuality between the sexes which they see as an image of Christ and his church, and which reaches back to the 'image of God' in the Genesis stories. These Christians have been seeking quietly to understand the implications of such beliefs in the light of history, particularly the history of the church.[1]*

The first Assembly of the WCC in Amsterdam 'supported the suggestion that a permanent commission of men and women be formed, which would relate to the general structure of the World Council and co-ordinate and encourage activities related to the question of women's ministry.'[2]

The Central Committee meeting in Chichester, England in 1949 set up an official Commission on the Life and Work of Women in the Church with Sarah Chakko of India in the chair and Kathleen Bliss of England as secretary. Throughout the 1950s and 1960s the WCC work on women's issues continued. It was, however, only at the Nairobi Assembly that women really began to break through. For the first time they were present in significant numbers, and a plenary presentation was allotted to them. The issues poured out and the Study on the Community of Women and Men was set up to consider them more deeply.

The World Council of Churches and the ordination of women

Among the issues raised at the Nairobi Assembly was that of the ordination of women. The WCC had begun the 1970s by holding a small Consultation on the Ordination of Women in Cartigny, Geneva, from 21–26 September 1970. This meeting brought together twenty-five participants from six continents representing eight different traditions. They included Roman Catholics and one Orthodox bishop. A report of the Conference was edited by Brigalia Bam of the Women's Desk with the title 'What is Ordination Coming to?' The British participants were Mary Levison and Margaret Forrester, both deaconesses from the Church of Scotland, and Alan Webster, an Anglican priest who was Dean of Norwich. Among the WCC staff present was Dr Ian Fraser, a Presbyterian from the Church of Scotland who commented trenchantly:

> *What seems lacking to me is a positive theological case for ordaining women. It is agreed that the negative work has been done well, but it is believed that this clearing away of the brushwood of bad biblical exegesis and bad theological thinking is insufficient. Can we then prepare a theologically argued case for ordaining women as part of the necessary pattern of the Church? I believe not. We can produce no positive theological case for ordaining Scotsmen – by a clear oversight on the part of God, they were not represented among the apostolic band: but the extension of the Church to the Gentiles cleared the way for the ordaining of people of all nations. The same extension of the Church to total humanity is, surely, the basis for opening the possibility of ordination to total humanity.[3]*

At the back of the Report a small chart set out the position on the Ordination of Women in the member churches of the WCC. This revealed that at that time 72 member churches of the WCC did ordain women and 143 did not. In 1970 no Anglican churches ordained women and of course no Roman Catholic, Old Catholic or Orthodox. Four Baptist churches ordained women and eight did not, while one agreed to the principle but had not put it into practice. Ten Lutheran churches ordained women and twenty did not. Seven Methodist churches ordained women, while ten did not, and one more had agreed to the principle but had not yet put it into practice. Perhaps more surprisingly, 23 Reformed churches ordained women and 33 did not – a clear sign of the influence of cultural factors. Five Congregational churches had ordained women, three had agreed in principle and two did not. Behind these statistics stretched years of struggle and pain as well as of change and joy. Where did it all begin?

A Canadian preparatory paper focused on the dynamic of the church itself:

> *On Easter Morn there were eleven men 'set apart' (but surely not formally ordained to a Ministry of Word and Sacraments in the congregation), but there were no three-level ministries, no congregations, no 'church' as we know it, no scriptures, no rituals, ecclesiastical structures, canons, or forms of any kind. All we have was one day proposed by or grew out of the needs of a particular situation in a particular age as something 'new' – was examined prayerfully, tested theologically, and, under God, judged to be 'good' for its time; thus did tradition grow and continuity become established.*[4]

Women in church history

One might go back to those eleven men, but one might also go back to the women who went to the tomb very early on that first Easter morning. As Elisabeth Moltmann-Wendel said in the public dialogue with her husband at the Sheffield International Conference on the Community of Women and Men in the Church in 1981:

> *Church history begins when a few women set out to pay their last respects to their dead friend Jesus. It begins when, contrary to all reason and all hope, a few women identify themselves with a national traitor and do what they consider to be right, what in their eyes equals quality of life, namely loving one who has sacrificed his*

life, never abandoning him as dead. Church history begins when Jesus comes to them, greets them, lets them touch him just as he had touched and restored them in their lives. Church history begins when women are told to share with the men this experience, this life they now comprehend, this life their hands have touched . . .

This story as told by Matthew is generally known as the Easter appearance of the women but never as the beginning of church history. Officially church history begins with the mission of the men apostles and officially no women are present on that occasion.[5]

Of course there is a bit more to it in the New Testament. We do have hints of the role of Mary Magdalene and references to the women who helped St Paul. We even have the deacon Phoebe. What is more, in Peter's first Letter we are told that all baptised Christians belonged to the Royal Priesthood, and that certainly included women. Moreover, St Paul assured the Galatians that in baptism 'there is no such thing as Jew and Greek, slave and freeman, male or female; for you are all one person in Christ Jesus.' (Gal 3:28)

Yet when in due time the sacramental priesthood came to be established there was no place in it for women. Baptised into Christ they may be, members of the Priesthood of all Believers they may be, but in the sacramental priesthood they apparently could not be. Even the deaconess order died out – their role in clothing female adult baptism candidates passed away as infant baptism became the norm. Only in religious orders did women find an official place in the church – and sometimes an escape from domineering husbands or perpetual childbearing. Change had to wait for many centuries.

Women as missionaries

The modern ecumenical movement in the churches was given its stimulus by the missionary movement, and it is fascinating to note that long before the British churches were prepared to admit women to their formal ministries in this country, they (or their missionary societies) were quite happy to send them abroad as missionaries. They went as women married to clergy; as single women teachers or nurses; and eventually as doctors. Many of them lived in appalling conditions and many died young as a result of fever. Examples of these women can be seen in the window near the lady chapel in Liverpool Anglican Cathedral, where one of the stations was held in the pilgrimage service during the conference which began the WCC's Ecumenical Decade – Churches in Solidarity with Women, in 1988.

Women and ministry in the churches

The Society of Friends believes that God speaks directly to the heart of every man and woman. They have long given women an equal part with men. Early in the 19th century Elizabeth Fry combined her Quaker responsibilities with work in women's prisons.

The Salvation Army pioneered female equality in its organisation and ministry. Catherine Booth, the wife of the Army's founder, took up many social concerns, and co-operated with the notable feminist and reformer Josephine Butler. She combined this work with a preaching ministry. She was an excellent preacher who drew crowds to listen to her. She silenced criticism of women becoming officers in the Salvation Army by saying, 'Souls have no sex.' She also wrote: 'Who can tell what God can do by any man or woman however timid, however faint, if only fully given up to him.' In the Salvation Army at least women were now in recognised official service, and married couples exercised a joint ministry. This did bring some problems but it was a great breakthrough. Other early 'Hallelujah Lassies' included Pamela Shepherd who preached and worked in the Welsh valleys, and Florence Soper who married Bramwell Booth.

Women were not admitted into the formal ministries of the other Christian denominations in Britain until the 20th century (although the first woman whose ordination was formally recognised by her church was an American Congregationalist, Revd Antoinette Brown, ordained in 1853). It is fascinating to observe the same pattern in all the churches. First women were sent as missionaries. Then they were allowed into some unofficial ministries and then into some 'second rank' subordinate ministries such as deaconess. Finally they were admitted into the ordained ministries of Word, Sacrament and Leadership. There were always arguments over the nature of the biblical evidence; issues of headship; the biblical injunction for silence of women and questions of authority. The nearer one got to concepts of 'priesthood', the more bitter the struggle became, as arguments from tradition and gut feelings about sexuality became mixed up with biblical questions. The Congregational Church was the first to allow women to exercise an unofficial ministry, but no woman was recognised as an 'accredited minister'. As early as 1908 the question of the position of such women was raised at a meeting of the Congregational Union Council, and a resolution was passed, stating that a woman who took the same theological training as a male candidate for ordination and who received a proper 'call' was entitled to recognition as a Congregational minister. Some of those who voted for this did so in the belief that such a case would never arise in practice. A woman named Constance Todd made sure it did. She was ordained to the Congregational ministry on 17 September 1917 at the King's Weigh House, a Congregational church in the west end of London. The following day she was married to Claud Coltman, who had been ordained with her at the same service. She wished to be an ordained minister in her own right before she became a married woman. (In October 1997 a special service was held in the City Temple church in London to celebrate the 80th Anniversary of Constance's ordination.)

Only the day before the Coltmans' ordination, Maude Royden had begun her assistant ministry in the City Temple, although as an Anglican she could not be a candidate for ordination. Maude was born in 1876 and was educated at Lady Margaret Hall, Oxford. She worked among the poor of Liverpool before moving to the City Temple. She said: 'The Church will never believe that women have a religious message until some of them get and take the opportunity to prove that they have. My taking it in a Nonconformist Church will ultimately lead, I believe, to other women being given it in the Church of England.' Many people went to hear Maude preach and she became a frequent broadcaster on religious topics.

A Congregational minister who also became famous as a broadcaster was Revd Elsie Chamberlain. She spent her whole life in the Congregational Church, first growing up in a devout family and then fulfilling her call to ministry. In 1946 she became the first woman chaplain to the forces. After leaving the Army chaplaincy she joined the BBC.

The Baptist Union of Great Britain (which does not include Scotland) was next. In 1890 the Deaconess Movement was started. In 1922 the first woman was accepted as a probationer minister by the Baptist Union. In 1925 the Baptist Union Council declared that Baptists saw no objection to women ministers and decided to include them in the Handbook as a separate list of 'women pastors'. In 1926 'women pastors' was changed to 'women ministers'. In 1966 the Baptist Union Council approved rules for deaconesses to apply to become ministers and in 1975 all active deaconesses became ministers. In 1975 women ministers were finally included in the main Accredited List in the Handbook.

The first English woman Presbyterian minister was ordained in 1921. One year later, the first, unsuccessful, attempt to open all offices to women came before the General Assembly of the Church of Scotland. It was to be almost fifty years before that proposal was finally accepted. In 1888, in response to pressure to recognise a distinctive women's ministry, the Order of Deaconesses was founded in the Church of Scotland. The Order was originally intended to be the apex of a 'pyramid', built on the foundations of the new Woman's Guild, and Lady Griselle Baillie was the first to be 'set apart' to organise work among women. In 1893 the Church of Scotland decided that faithful women would be a useful resource in its attempts to minister to areas of poverty and need. A plan to finance and appoint workers – to be called Parish Sisters – was introduced under the auspices of the Home Mission Committee.

In 1916 the United Free Church authorised the institution of a ministry to be known as Church Sister, for which women would be trained at the Women's Missionary College. In 1929, when the Church of Scotland and the United Free Church united, at the Union of the Churches there were in the Church of Scotland 62 deaconesses and 53 parish sisters and in the United Free Church about 60 church sisters. In 1949, revisions of arrangements for women's work brought them all into the diaconate. Any who had theological training equivalent to that of ministers could serve as assistants in parishes, conducting public worship and preaching. In 1954, on that basis, Mary Lusk was appointed to the Parish of St Michael's Inveresk at Musselburgh, and then in 1958 she was appointed tutor at St Colm's College (formerly the Women's Missionary College). In 1955 the Assembly discussed the whole question of the 'Order' of deaconesses on the basis of a report from a group containing no deaconesses!

At 2.30 pm on Saturday 26 May 1963 Mary Lusk stood at the bar of the General Assembly of the Church of Scotland to present her petition, which asked the Assembly to test what she believed to be her call to ministry. This was remitted to the Panel on Doctrine. In 1968, after votes in all the Presbyteries, the Church of Scotland agreed to open to women ordination to the ministry of Word and Sacrament, on the same basis as men. In 1969 Miss Catherine McConnachie was ordained by the Presbytery of Aberdeen. On St Andrew's Day 1978 Mary Lusk (who had married Fred Levison, a minister from Edinburgh, in 1965) was at last ordained herself. After serving the Church of Scotland in a faithful, diverse and distinguished ministry, both before and after her ordination, Mary Levison is now a Chaplain to the Queen – the first woman to be so appointed.

The Methodist Church also has a distinctive history of courageous and able women in ministry. Susannah Wesley, the mother of John and Charles, had led Bible studies, first in her kitchen and then in the church hall. Later she encouraged her sons to develop the work of lay preachers and quite early on in Methodism some of these were women. In common with other Protestant churches, Methodism also revived the ancient Deaconess

Order. In 1972 Conference agreed that there could be women ministers and in 1974 the first women were ordained. The Deaconess Order was abolished but then was later reinstituted for men and women.

The struggle for the ordination of women in the Anglican Communion

Ordination of women to the priesthood in the Church of England was the next to be achieved, but this struggle, part of a movement throughout the global Anglican Communion, was long and hard and bitter.

The very first woman to be ordained priest in the Anglican Communion was Li Tim Oi, a remarkable Chinese woman. She was born in 1907. Her father was a doctor who had given up medicine to become a headmaster. He was a Christian although he had two wives or, rather, an official wife and a mistress or concubine who lived in the same house. This concubine was Tim Oi's mother. Mr Li gave his newly born daughter an unusual name, Tim Oi meaning 'another much beloved daughter'. The Chinese tradition tended to undervalue and despise girls. Mr Li was determined to show that a daughter could be loved and cherished. His first daughter had died and so he gave his new daughter a name to express his joy. Some recent research in Britain has suggested that girls who are affirmed and encouraged by their fathers succeed best, and Tim Oi is a good example of this. Tim Oi was educated at Belilios Public School where she learnt about Florence Nightingale (from whom she took her own English name). She taught in a church school, graduated in theology at Union Theological College in Guangzhou, and became a lay worker. In 1940 she went to work in Macao where life became more difficult as the Japanese tightened their hold on South China. In 1941 she was ordained deacon. Macao belonged to Portugal and as the Portuguese were not at war with the Japanese it became a haven for refugees. Some of these went on to Taiwan where they met Bishop R.O. Hall, and they told him of the wonderful work Li Tim Oi was doing in Macao.

Some time later, Bishop Hall wrote to Li Tim Oi to ask her to travel to Xingxing to be ordained priest. After a difficult and dangerous journey they met and talked and prayed, and then Bishop Hall ordained her as the first Anglican priest. She then returned along the dangerous roads to Macao where she served as a priest for the rest of the war.

After the war Bishop Hall was strongly rebuked by the other Anglican bishops for what he had done. Tim Oi wrote to him with typical humility to say that she was a very tiny person, a mere worm, and she did not want to cause trouble for him. She promised not to exercise her priesthood but to work as though she were a deacon.

Li Tim Oi went back to China to work. She continued her ministry when the 'bamboo curtain' came down and suffered along with others in the Cultural Revolution during which all her books were burned and she had to do hard labour.

Yet her example bore fruit: in 1969 a resolution was put to the Hong Kong and Macao Diocesan Synod that two women should be ordained to the priesthood. This was accepted in 1971 and in the same year Bishop Baker told the Anglican Consultative Council meeting in Limuru in Kenya that he intended to conduct this ordination. The Anglican Consultative Council agreed that if he did so his church would still be regarded as part of the Anglican Communion and on Advent Sunday 1971 Jane Hwang and Joyce Bennet were ordained. In 1980 Joyce Bennet was able to travel to China and meet Li Tim Oi, who had been working there faithfully and rejoiced that the bamboo curtain was lifted and her priesthood was recognised once more. In 1981 Archbishop Ted Scott of Canada helped Li Tim Oi to leave China and join her relations in Canada. Tim Oi settled in Toronto where she worked as a priest. She visited England several times to give encouragement to women seeking ordination of the priesthood here. In January 1984 there were special celebrations in Toronto, London and Sheffield to mark the 40th anniversary of her ordination. Tim Oi came to stay with us in York and talked to a group of people in our home. When she left, my husband and I felt we had entertained a saint. She visited us once more but kept on writing until her death. I have photographs of her, and two pictures which she gave to me. I shall always treasure them. She was so humble and yet so strong and so devoted. She died in Canada on 27 February 1992, aged 84.

One by one, other parts of the Anglican Communion followed the example of Hong Kong and ordained women to the priesthood: America, Canada, New Zealand, Latin America, provinces in Africa – so the progress went on. In the United Church of South India there were women presbyters. Even the Irish went quietly ahead and ordained women to the priesthood. Their legislation also makes provision for women to be bishops when the time seems right. Grandmother Church of England lagged behind.

The struggle in England

The Order of Deaconesses was revived in England by Bishop Tait who, in 1862, ordained Elizabeth Ferrard as a deaconess. Successive Lambeth Conferences argued about their status, first saying that they were ordained and then that they were not, and finally that they were ordained but they were not deacons! They were in orders that were 'sui generis'. Eventually, after a long struggle, women were ordained deacon in 1987. The ordination in York Minster took place in March of that year on the day after the Zeebrugge ferry disaster. The service began with a solemn silent memorial for the dead but then moved on in joy, with Archbishop Habgood telling us all to offer a vote of thanks to Phoebe! After the ordination we had a huge party in our home in Minster Close for supporters of the Movement for the Ordination of Women (MOW).

MOW was formed in 1979 as the result of a meeting which had taken place in the Church Commissioners' Board Room in 1978, on the invitation of Betty Ridley, Third Church Estates Commission. The meeting in 1978 was called because many of us who were on General Synod realised that we would not make any progress without a more direct campaign. The motion to ordain women, which had been proposed by Hugh Montefiore, Bishop of Birmingham, had failed even to get a simple majority in the House of Clergy and had only just scraped through in the House of Laity. I had been present at the Synod vote, I was present at the founding meeting of MOW, and I played an active part in stimulating the growth of MOW in the Northern Province. The first meeting to encourage this growth took place in our vicarage at Ecclesfield near Sheffield. The general story of the struggle for the ordination of women in the Church of England became my story, or – perhaps more accurately – my story had become part of a larger whole.

My vocation

I had come to believe that I had a vocation to the priesthood when I was in my teens, but of course I was told that this was completely impossible. I was brought up in a High Anglo Catholic church where my faith was nurtured and my vocation spurned. Still very uncertain about what to do, I went to Oxford to read history at Lady Margaret Hall – the College of Maude Royden and Mary Levison. After prelims many of my men friends changed to read theology, but I was told that women were not mature enough to read theology as their first degree! I read history and then was offered the chance to read a second degree in theology but no grants were available. With wonderful help from my parents I read a one-year theology diploma instead. My Doctrine tutor, David Jenkins of Queens College, was amazingly encouraging. 'Don't worry,' he said, 'the diploma Doctrine course is much more useful. If you were reading a degree you would get stuck in the Fathers!'

During my theology year I went for a selection conference and was accepted to train as a 'Lady Worker' in the Church of England. On reflection I felt I could not face all the limitations and frustrations which would be involved in that work. I felt called to priesthood and not to 'lady workership'. I do so admire those women who moved in and worked as 'lady/women workers', and later as deaconesses. With courage and patience they pushed back the boundaries. I could not have done it. I would either have exploded or have been destroyed and embittered by frustration.

Instead I taught RE in Lancashire, married and taught RE in

London and Nottinghamshire and in 1965, at the age of 29, was elected as a Member of Church Assembly for the Diocese of Southwell, whose prophetic bishop, Dr Russel Barry, gave me every support and encouragement. He had a Bishop's Council, of which I was a member, long before they became part of the official structure of the Church of England.

As a member of Church Assembly I joined in the debate on 'Women and Holy Orders' – a report which was published in 1966. I remember in one speech saying that I did not seek orders for myself but for others. I sat down and thought, 'That is not true,' and then I thought, 'Oh yes it is.' I firmly told God that he had had his chance with me. His rotten old church could only take me as a lady worker and that was no good. I would work so that others could be priests but he had had his chance with me and that was that!

I pushed my own sense of vocation right into the background and got into the fray. It was the only way I could cope. So I spoke in debates when I was called. I was present at the meeting in the Church Commissioners' board room when MOW was born. I held a meeting in our vicarage in Ecclesfield (Sheffield) to launch MOW in the Northern Province and I travelled around the Northern Province persuading each diocese to appoint a diocesan representative.

The synodical system in the Church of England came into being in 1970 and the ordination of women went on being discussed at all levels: deanery, diocesan and general. Time after time we went over the same ground and the same arguments. In 1985 I took over the convenership of the MOW Synod Steering Group. This group did lots of hard work planning for Synod debates: visualising what amendments might be brought by the opponents, persuading people to send in their names and prepare speeches, being ready to speak if necessary. It was hard, laborious and painstaking but it paid off.

At the 1989 November debate, which culminated in approval being given to the draft measure, all our careful planning bore fruit. As if miraculously, the chairman called our chosen speakers. On the final vote the measure was sent to the dioceses with large majorities in favour. When we came out of the Synod, newspaper placards proclaimed the breaching of the Berlin Wall and the front pages of the evening papers carried pictures of people dancing on the top of that wall. We felt we had begun to breach the wall of partition between men and women in the priesthood.

Meanwhile God had caught up with me. For seven years I had been teaching on the Northern Ordination Course, an ecumenical course training mature men and women for the ministry with sessions in the evenings and at weekends. I found the work deeply fulfilling and felt that my work in Synod for the ordination of women was personalised as a struggle for my women students. They would not let me get off the hook. They pressed me to jump in and join them, and so early in 1990 I went back to a selection centre run by the Advisory Council for the Church's Ministry (ACCM). I was accepted for training as a deacon with a view to possible ordination to the priesthood if it became available.

In July 1990 I left General Synod, where I had served for 25 years on Standing Committee, Church of England Liturgical Commission and as representative on the Central Committee of the WCC, as well as on numerous other committees. At that session the Archbishop of York mentioned by name many people who were not standing for election again and thanked them for their work. He never mentioned my name. I must admit it hurt and my family have never forgiven him for it. I later stood for election to the House of Clergy – once in York and twice in Durham. I was not elected. That hurt too. I would have loved to get back on Synod, not for the honour but in order to battle a bit more for the church to become a truly inclusive community. It was not to be, and my energies have been redirected elsewhere.

My ordination to the diaconate

In June 1991 I was ordained deacon in York Minster. A friend said that as I processed in with the others he looked at my face and thought that I was still deeply troubled, wondering whether this really was the right step. As we walked out he felt that my face was serene and confident. The right thing had been done.

The priesthood open at last

When the measure for the ordination of women to the priesthood came back to General Synod for final approval in November 1992, I was asked by the BBC to be available for comment on the result. I spent the morning sitting in the Gallery of Church House listening to the debate – I had been lucky in the ballot for tickets. In the afternoon I watched the debate on TV in the studio which had been set up in Church House. I had discussed with my daughters beforehand how I would react if the vote failed. I had said that I was sure that I would burst into tears. They said, 'Oh you mustn't do that. You must have a speech ready for if it fails and put on a brave face.' So I did. In the event it passed and I nearly burst into tears because of that!

When the vote was announced my brain just would not work out the right percentages to discover whether we had the necessary two thirds majority. Then one of the technicians turned to me with a broad grin on his face and said, 'You've got it!' At that moment the cameras in the square outside took over, and out there in Church House Yard there was a scene of joy almost beyond belief. As those outside took in the tremendous fact of the decision, they broke into embracing and tears – tears of joy. In fact someone said afterwards that they had never seen so many grown men weeping, because, of course, there were many faithful men among the supporters in the Movement for the Ordination of Women.

Then the cameras were thrown back from those scenes of unbelief and yet delirious joy and excitement outside to those of us who were in the studio, and we had to make our comment. I managed to overcome my urge to burst into tears, and expressed my joy and delight that after all these years this had happened; my thanks to my daughters and my family who had shared in the struggle so long; and my sense that the whole world had burst out singing. The words that came into my mind were those of Siegfried Sassoon's poem about Armistice Day, which concludes 'and the singing will never be done'.

But then I turned to the principal of Pusey House, something that wasn't planned, but which I just did spontaneously. I put my hand on his hand, and said that we needed him: 'Please don't go. Stay with us; we need you.' It was an action which received a variety of responses afterwards, but I can only say that it came naturally from the situation in which we found ourselves that day, and it expressed something that I very sincerely felt, although I never realised just how high the cost would be.

When I got home to York that night I found that a card had already been pushed through my door by one of my Roman Catholic priest friends, expressing his joy and delight, and his hope that his church may follow in the footsteps of the Anglican Church before too long. The next morning Nicole Fischer rang up from the Ecumenical Centre in Geneva to offer her congratulations. I said to her, 'I am sorry all this has taken away our energy from the Ecumenical Decade.' She replied, 'Jean, this *is* part of your effort for the Decade.'

After I had returned home I had been interviewed on the phone by a reporter from the *York Evening Press*. At the very end of his interview he asked me about the Archdeacon of York's 'package' – his view that ordaining women was all part of a package to ordain gays and call God 'Mother'. I spoke very carefully and in a balanced way, saying that I had some concerns for lesbian and homosexual people and I also would like to see some changes in the language of the liturgy, but I felt that we must do it very gently and carefully, and certainly did not think that this was part of any package, or any subject for a new campaign.

The next day the *Evening Press* came out with a banner headline: 'Minster deacon now calls for new campaign to change the language of worship and ordain gays and lesbians as priests'. For the next few days there was merry hell to play, with vitriolic letters pouring in to me and the Dean, who made it clear to me that he did not want a woman priest in the Minster. The main things that kept me sane in these days were the presence of my brother-in-law, who saw things in a dispassionate but supportive way, and the wonderful letters I received from my students. When my younger daughter phoned, I told her about the foul letters. She said, 'Haven't you had any nice ones?' I said, 'Yes of course I have, especially from my students.' She said, 'Well look at them and put the others in the waste paper basket.'

In the end the Archbishop of York's press officer intervened and compelled the *Evening Press* to publish a statement by me and the incident was closed from their point of view. The harm had, however, been done. I have to say that in all this unpleasant situation the Archbishop of York and the Bishop of Selby were very understanding and helpful.

The backlash

In the weeks that followed, however, it was clear that the major attention of the Archbishop and the rest of the senior staff was being given to those people who opposed the ordination of women, and who were now screaming out aloud their pain and their horror and their terror. The attitude of most of the senior staff became really hurtful and unsupportive to the women deacons in the diocese. Within the setting of York Minster I also found a distinct change in attitude. The Dean and the other canons had been reasonably supportive of me whilst I was Deacon. I don't think any of them had expected the vote to go in favour of the ordination of women to the priesthood. Although my husband and one of the other canons were wholeheartedly in favour of ordination, the general attitude and atmosphere of the place changed to one of disapproval and distinct coolness.

It became increasingly obvious to me that I was a *persona non grata* at the Minster. My husband also became more and more unhappy about his role there. He was 67. Officially he could stay there until he was 70 but that was only going to bring strain and unhappiness. We needed to have one of us earning a full-time salary because my husband, having entered the priesthood late, would not be eligible for a full pension, our younger daughter was still at university, and our elder daughter needed some help with her financial affairs. My husband and I decided that I would apply for a full-time post and if I got one he would retire.

The move to Durham

In June 1993 I began work in Durham as Anglican Diocesan Ecumenical Officer and County Ecumenical Officer. I was licensed at the Diocesan Synod. I went out to the front and read the necessary legal oaths. Bishop David Jenkins looked at me seriously during these oaths, but all the time there was a twinkle in his eyes which he never quite loses. After the official part of the business, Bishop David prayed for my work using the Alternative Service Book collect for unity, which he changed to make it inclusive. When he had finished the other prayers he took my hand again. I felt that at last I had come home to work with a bishop who understood some of my vision and my longings and who was entirely sympathetic not only to the cause of the ordination of women to the priesthood, but to the other issues surrounding it such as inclusive language, the nature of the priesthood and the whole nature of God. The weeks that followed bore this out.

We were so lucky as women in the Diocese of Durham. Bishop David made money available for us to meet as women to thrash out the issues. He encouraged us to be adventurous. He supported, loved and challenged. When it came to my pre-priesting interview, we met in his untidy, comfortable, friendly study where he greeted me with his usual twinkle and said, 'Well, what is there left to say?' We then sat down and reflected together on the wonderful and mysterious ways of God which had brought us together again in one round circle. Many years before Bishop David had been my Doctrine tutor. Now something which at that time neither of us could have expected was going to happen. He was going to ordain me before he retired. I felt this was a great privilege and a great joy.

I am eternally grateful to God, with whom I often wrestle, that along the mysterious path of life where the going is often so dark, She has brought me on occasions to sit in places of stimulation, or of tranquillity and joy. That afternoon in Bishop David's study, in Auckland Castle, I knew one such moment of 'arriving' and the challenge of setting out once more on the way ahead, stimulated by Bishop David's conversation, and trusting in God who had called me. At our ordination retreat, Bishop David gave two addresses: one entitled 'Why the ordination of women is the most wonderful thing that has happened since Creation' and the other entitled 'Why the ordination of women does not matter a damn'. In other words, to ordain women is to affirm that women are truly made fully in the image of God – but don't you women dare to get clericalised, for ordination is to service, not to power!

Ordination to the priesthood

Thirty-eight of us were ordained on two consecutive days in May 1994. I was ordained on the Sunday – Trinity Sunday – which was also the fortieth anniversary of Bishop David's own ordination to the priesthood. To mark the occasion we gave him forty red roses after the service and joined in the laughter and the tears. Chris Sterry, a friend with whom I had taught on the Northern Ordination Course, said that he had never been to an ordination of such 'aweful' holiness in the very best sense of the word. 'If anyone could call down the Holy Spirit,' he said, 'Bishop David could.'

Most people spend the night before their ordination in prayer and reflection. I was up most of the night preparing lunch for the next day, once all our visitors had been tucked up in bed. Still, it was good. I can always meditate best when I am doing something. By that time our house looked like a flower show. I had received flowers from so many people, including a wonderful bouquet in papal colours from the former and the current secretaries of Cardinal Danneels of Mechelin, Brussels, whom we had got to know through the special York Minster/Mechelin link begun by Cardinal Mercier and Lord Halifax. I also received a beautiful arrangement of flowers sent by Bishop Desmond Tutu and his wife Leah. There was a card signed by all the members of the Central Committee of the Conference of European Churches, who at that time were meeting in Bossey, near Geneva. Professor Papaderos of the Greek Orthodox Church said, 'This does not mean that I approve of the ordination of women but I want to send greetings to Jean.' Who says that the ordination of women to the priesthood is ecumenically divisive?

First Eucharist

There had been no service in Brancepeth that Sunday morning but we had our Trinity Sunday Eucharist at night. Chris and I had often shared the Presidency of the Eucharist at the Northern Ordination Course – I did the Ministry of the Word and he took over at the Peace. That night I was to preside over it all, and he was to preach. It was a wonderful and humbling privilege to celebrate my first Eucharist in that ancient parish church with the shades of Bishop Cousin and other liturgical scholars around me. When I began the Eucharistic Prayer I felt I would not be able to get through it without collapsing into tears but with Chris standing by me and holding the book and willing me on I got through. Never will leading the people in making Eucharist lose its humbling thrill, but never again will it be such an awe-inspiring privilege as that first time.

The Act of Synod

After those wonderful days, we settled down to the routine of work and began to face the implications of the Act of Synod which the bishops had devised and which the Archbishop of York had pressed through General Synod. The measure which made provision for the ordination of women to the priesthood gave ample protection to the consciences of those who were opposed. Parishes need not receive women priests and bishops need not ordain them. The opposition had, however, pressed for more and the bishops foolishly had given in. The Act of Synod made provision for the consecration of special Episcopal Visitors (flying bishops as they came to be known) who would minister to those parishes who would be entitled to vote not to receive their own bishop for confirmations, etc., if he had ordained women.

I opposed this Act of Synod from the start. It was heretical and non-ecumenical, and absolutely unacceptable to women priests who were being made expendable in this way. Either the Synod had voted to ordain women or it had not. One could not have it both ways; nor could one treat women in a way that would be completely unacceptable if applied to black men. I was no longer on General Synod and so I could not oppose it there, but I signed the petition against it and went to see Bishop David to express my anger. For an hour I threw every argument against him and he took it. At last in exasperation I asked him why on earth he had voted for it. He replied that he must recognise that there were faithful parish priests in his diocese who, with integrity, opposed the ordination of women. If they would not accept his ministry if he ordained women, then he must share the pain of rejection experienced by the women and make canonical provision for those opposed to receive the ministry of another bishop. He felt that this was a way for the Church of England to show compassion to the world.

I tried to accept what he said but could not. As events have turned out I think Bishop David has regrets. What happened was that the 'flying bishops' peddled a theology of taint: some of them went around persuading clergy to join a separate Chapter of Our Lady and St Cuthbert, and not to meet in Chapter with their fellow clergy. Bishop Michael Turnbull, who succeeded Bishop David, tried to build bridges by inviting the Bishop of Beverley to join the Senior Staff Meetings, and so on; but if he gave an inch, the 'Forward in Faith' group wanted to take a mile.

In November 1997 Bishop Edwin Barnes came out into the open and demanded a 'Third Province' with over a thousand parishes passing into the hands of what had come to be known (quite illegally) as 'the other integrity'. The Church of England does not exist for itself but for the people of England, and bewildered parishioners do not want to pass to some other integrity of which they know nothing. Our whole mission as a church is being marred by this bigoted group and it is high time that the House of Bishops got their act together and dealt with the issue – even to the point of telling these people to go if necessary.

In her book *Wrestling with the Church* Mary Levison says that she has never had to campaign or to fight with her church. I, along with my sister priests, have had to campaign and also fight with our church long and hard. Yet I love the Church of England with every fibre of my being and it is because I love it, with all its faults, that I am also free to be completely ecumenically open. But it is the Church of England – not the Church of Churchy People; nor of bigoted, unreconstructed men; nor of brainwashed women. We must live up to our demanding responsibilities as the Church of the Nation and not be turned into an inward-looking, warring sect.

My journey continues

The situation in the Diocese of Durham has got worse since I left and I do feel for the women there. I did not leave because of 'Forward in Faith' but for family reasons. My husband never settled there and Bishop Michael decided that he must retire from being a non-stipendiary (NSM) priest in Brancepeth at seventy. Bishop Michael suggested that I should give up the county part of my job, keep the Anglican part and have a parish of my own. This I would have loved after the long, long wait but sadly the offer had come too late. Ralph, my husband, felt that he could not face being at the centre of parish life any more, even if the parish was mine. At first I was angry, feeling that I had supported him for years and now he could not support me. Then I decided that I could not go on being angry after 36 years of marriage, and so I applied for the post of Associate Secretary for the Community of Women and Men in the Church, at the Council of Churches for Britain and Ireland (CCBI). Now I exercise my priesthood at some weekends and in some lunch hours at St John's, Waterloo Road, which is a great joy. Meanwhile I practise a little gentle boat-rocking on behalf of my Roman Catholic and Orthodox sisters, and also seek to build up the Community of Women and Men in Church and Society. One of the joys is to be back working once more with the Women's Sub Unit of the WCC.

When Mary Levison wrestled to become a minister only one skeleton fell out of the cupboard – that of ordination. In the Church of England all the skeletons have fallen out at once: priesthood, ordination, inclusive language, the motherhood of God, issues of sexuality. It has made the battle long and bitter; but it has enabled us to put all our cards on the table and to have a chance to break masculine moulds of ministry.

Many of the women ordained in the Free Churches were ordained to a masculine model of ministry and are now entering into the second stage of their struggle. This is clear for example in the foundation (after twenty years of ordination) of the Forum of Women Ministers in the Methodist Church – seeking to minister as women and not as imitation men.

The reports of the WCC Team Visits of 'Living Letters' to assess the results of the *Ecumenical Decade of Churches in Solidarity with Women* have found the same phenomenon all the world over. Some churches still refuse to ordain women, for example the Orthodox and Roman Catholic Churches, but many more do now accept the ordained ministry of women than in 1971 when the first report on ordination was produced. There has been a tremendous growth of women pastors in the Lutheran Churches, for example, and several of the Scandinavian countries now have Lutheran women bishops.

The image of God

Even where churches do ordain women, however, they are not universally welcomed, and many still find the higher positions closed to them. In the Church of England, for example, we shall need new legislation before women can be consecrated as bishops and that battle is going to be a painful one. At the Lambeth Conference in 1998 there were only eleven women bishops from Canada, New Zealand and America amongst hundreds of men.

The Living Letters Final Report of the WCC Team Visits recommends that:

> *We ask Churches . . . where they already ordain women, to affirm them clearly by providing vocational opportunities and practical support to help congregations accept women pastors with joy and*

> *gratitude, making sure in the case of married women pastors that their placement takes the whole family's situation into account.[6]*

The same report also says:

> *We therefore call on the churches to understand that women and men are persons created in God's image and to God's glory and thus that the community of women and men – a new community of all persons across gender, racial, ethnic, class and economic lines in partnership and solidarity with each other – is of the essence of the church and its mission today.[7]*

In a way we are back to where we started. As it celebrates the 50th Anniversary of its first Assembly (held in Amsterdam, 1948), the WCC is still trying to convince its member churches that women really are made in the image of God. When will the churches truly accept this and live it? When indeed! With the prophets of old we cry, 'Lord, how long?'

POST SCRIPT

After the Festival in Harare in November 1998 which ended the Ecumenical Decade – Churches in Solidarity with Women, a letter was sent to the Eighth Assembly of the World Council of Churches which was to follow. In spite of strong objections at revision stage this mentioned the ordination of women as a problem along with ethical issues such as abortion, divorce and human sexuality. Afterwards I protested strongly about this to Aruna Gnanadason at the Women's Desk, saying that we ordained women are tired of still being thought of as a problem. She said that it was done out of sensitivity to the Orthodox, but she also raised the matter with Konrad Raiser, the WCC Secretary, and with Alan Faulkner of the Faith and Order Commission, reminding them of their long-standing commitment to follow up on the Community of Women and Men Study Process. It is hoped to have a consultation early in 2000. So we continue!

Notes and references

1   Susannah Herzel, *A Voice of Women*. World Council of Churches, Geneva, 1981, page not numbered.

2   Ibid., p 10

3   Brigalia Bam (ed.), *What is Ordination Coming to?* Report of a Consultation on the Ordination of Women held in Cartigny, Geneva, Switzerland 21–26 September 1970. World Council of Churches, Geneva, 1971, p 19.

4   Ibid., p 3.

5   Constance Parvey (ed.), *The Community of Women and Men in the Church*. The Sheffield Report, WCC, Geneva, 1983, p 29.

6   Nicole Fischer-Duchable (ed.), *Living Letters*, A Report of Visits to the Churches during the Ecumenical Decade – Churches in Solidarity with Women. World Council of Churches, Geneva, 1997, p 49.

7   Ibid., p 49.

3 *'I have a dream for Leith': the story of one woman's remarkable ministry*

Elizabeth Wardlaw

I was baptised and brought up in St Ninian's Church of Scotland, Corstorphine, on the west side of Edinburgh. I went all through Sunday School and Bible Class as a pupil, then taught in all the departments and became leader in the Juniors. I took my vows and became a member of Christ's church as a teenager. From an early age, I felt called to be a minister. One summer, on holiday at my grandparents' farm, as the custom was, the family walked to the church about a mile away. I remember the minister, the Revd Mr Rae, preached on Jesus calling his disciples, saying, 'Now if you feel Jesus is calling you to follow Him, just say so now, or go home, kneel down quietly in a place by yourself and give your life to Jesus.' I did just that in my grandma's little bedroom upstairs. From that time, I felt called to be Christ's minister. But how? The Church of Scotland did not ordain women for the ministry in those days. However, parents of children in New Deer would tell their children 'to stick in at their lessons' and that's what I did for the following years.

I was a pupil at Corstorphine Primary, New Deer and Boroughmuir Schools. They were all co-ed schools, so boys and girls learned together, played together and supported each other's team games. It was the same at university and in hockey I played goalie where I could use my feet rather than a stick, as I had been born with no right hand or forearm. I had also been a prefect and head girl at school and my university colleagues put me up for the Students Representative Council. I fought the election for first year arts women and won. I was elected Assistant Secretary of the SRC, Junior President for three years running, and editor of the Students' Handbook, and I played in the first XI hockey team for several

years and won a Blue. I was also President of the Women's Union
and the Women's Athletic Club.

I graduated MA and went on to New College (the Faculty of
Divinity at Edinburgh University) to do a Bachelor of Divinity
degree. New College was used for training Church of Scotland
candidates for the ministry. It was predominantly a male domain in
those days and there was a large number of male postgraduates
from America. In my year, there was a large group of candidates
for the Church of Scotland ministry. There were also Irish,
Australian and German students, training for the ministry for their
national churches, but doing the BD course as a university course.
Some ex-service students also shared our classes. I am happy to
report that the students accepted me as a colleague and a friend.
Some years previously, critics had said that women had not the
ability to take a BD degree. Doctor Elizabeth Hewat had graduated
in 1926 as the first woman Edinburgh University BD: so a woman's
intellectual ability had been proved! I used to tell this little story to
the many elders' groups and woman's guilds throughout Scotland
who asked me to speak on 'Women in the Ministry':

A young lad stands before his father, who is studying the
lad's report card.
   Father – 'Second in class, John. Who beat you?'
   John – 'A girl.'
   Father – 'You don't mean to tell me a mere girl beat you.'
   John – 'Girls are not so mere nowadays, father.'

In those days students had grants for tuition fees. Church of
Scotland students could sit an examination for a bursary and be
allocated a bursary. As I was not accepted as a Church of Scotland
student, I had not been permitted to sit the examination at the
beginning of the course, so did not have a bursary. In my second
year, I learned that most of the students had bursaries or legacies
left for students at New College. My colleagues also had grants and
book grants too. I had neither. So I asked my professor if there was
any possibility of my getting a legacy or bursary. He replied, 'Well,

do you really need one? I don't want to get you a grant/legacy just to buy ribbons for your hair.' I did not wear ribbons in my hair. Perhaps he was being humorous! But I was badly hurt and left the table where we were sitting to have a good cry. My father and mother were sacrificing to help me through college and I was teaching drama at a school, thanks to my elocution teacher handing over the appointment so that I could make some money to help put me through college. I can sympathise now with poor students, unemployed people and all kinds of disadvantaged people for I know how they feel when they have to ask for help. Far better that the help is given graciously and fairly and the self-esteem of the person in need is built up and left intact. I am happy to say I did get a legacy and happier still that I learned to appreciate the spiritual stature of that professor as the years passed.

At the end of third year, before we sat the final BD exams, the professors used to ask students to their homes for a discussion and buffet supper. Only two professors invited me and made me most welcome. At the end of term, students received their certificates of duly performed work in their classes. New College also gave a grade for each subject. The final year students were telling each other the grades they had gained in each subject. 'I got an A in New Testament,' said one. 'I got a B in Hebrew,' said another. I didn't even get a certificate. I was upset. One of the sensitive students of my class noticed and had a quiet word with the professor responsible. 'Oh, Miss S,' he addressed me, 'you haven't got a certificate. Well, of course you can have one. Come to my room later and I'll have it ready for you.' I graduated BD that summer but was not licensed for the ministry. What was I to do now?

Six years before, I had met an ex-service science student. He was tall, dark and handsome. He played football and started the mid-week league for soccer at the university, allowing more people to play in the mid-week Inter-Faculty Cup League; and he was captain of the football club and the first XI, which won the East of Scotland Amateur League. He also won a Blue for soccer and started the Spartans Club for graduates. He had now graduated and had started teaching. We had been engaged for a year and were to be married after my graduation. It was he who suggested we should perhaps try missionary work. I would be the missionary, he would teach. We had an interview and the mission official was very excited. 'Yes, the missionary field could use a teacher of science anywhere: just right in all qualifications – and sport and music too! You play the violin, the cello, the sax, clarinet, you have a Glenn Miller style band, and a ceilidh band! You would be accepted.'

'But what about my wife?' asked Elliot. 'Oh, she would go with you, but she would not get a job. She would go as your wife,' replied the interviewer. (Incidentally, the Church of Scotland practice in those days did not even name the wives: they appeared as an asterisk after their husband's name on the List of Missionaries). Elliot replied, 'I am teaching at James Clark's School in Dumbiedykes. It is as missionary a situation as possible. It is my wife who is called to the ministry. I feel I've got my missionary post now, at the school.' One door had closed.

'Well, perhaps you should try to be a deaconess,' said my friends at college. The Order of Deaconesses was, at that time, becoming more fully recognised in the Church of Scotland, so I applied. Sitting before a matronly lady, I was getting on quite well when suddenly she noticed the engagement ring on my finger. 'Oh, are you engaged?' she asked. 'Yes', I replied. 'Are you going to be married?'

I was astonished. What young woman wears an engagement ring from her fiancé and doesn't plan to be married? 'Yes', I replied, 'in a few weeks.' Her response was, 'We don't have married ladies in the Deaconess Order, only single ladies and widows.' Young as I was, with a handsome young man full of love for me and I for him, I wanted to be neither a widow nor single. Another closed door.

'Well,' said my colleagues, 'why don't you join another denomination?' I had been brought up in the Church of Scotland from baptism as a baby. I really did not want to leave the Church of Scotland, where I felt I belonged. Elliot and I discussed the future. 'What about going to Moray House to train as a teacher?'

suggested Elliot. 'You might get a religious education post, only there are very few at this time and they are all in private schools.' I confess I never wanted to be a teacher, but I remember that great missionary, Lesslie Newbiggin, telling us that he was destined to go into the family business when he really wanted to be a missionary. When he was willing to let God lead him, when he obeyed God, the way opened up for him to be a missionary: and what a fine missionary he was to become. He helped form the United Church of North India, which holds various denominations in India in one family.

Elliot and I prayed about our situation, and after our marriage I went to Moray House as a trainee teacher. I had to do pre-college teaching and was fortunate enough to work under an excellent teacher. She demonstrated an example of class control which was new but very encouraging. All the pupils were interested and worked voluntarily at their own rate. What a fine teacher she was. When I had finished at teacher training college, I got a temporary job at James Clark School. I took the classes of a male teacher whose forte was teaching very tough lads. His discipline was very strong and he was a very able teacher. At that time, the belt was in use throughout schools, but I was determined I would not resort to it. These huge boys thought my way of teaching literature – for example, dramatising Shakespeare – was great fun. It meant there was a bit of noise in the classroom, especially as they acted out the rude mechanical scenes of *A Midsummer Night's Dream* with Bottom wearing the ass's head. A neighbouring teacher thought I was not coping and came 'to my aid' by entering the room, taking the stage, marching the noisiest fellows outside and strapping them hard. That was the end of drama with that class.

Fortunately, I was successful in getting a permanent post at Ainslie Park School under that great pioneer headteacher, Norman Murchieson. 'Experiment in your teaching,' he would say. 'These youngsters are in a new area. They have come from the slums of Edinburgh and Leith. Help them to learn in any way you think will work, and let them join in anything you can to extend their

learning, their imagination, their vision of what they might do now
or what they might do when they leave school. And I'll give you as
many classes for religious education as I can,' he finished. My
classes were of mixed ability but they enjoyed my methods. For
example, they loved being reporters and writing up about football
matches like a newspaper writer, or pretending to do live
interviews on the television or radio, reports on a match or motor
racing, or reading the news. They also liked me to tell or read a
story or poem: they would draw a picture of it or rewrite the story
or change the ending to their version. Sometimes they would act.
In a year, the classes had written a Bible Pageant with scenes of
Old Testament stories which they acted in their own 'lingo'. This
was years before *Joseph and His Amazing Technicolor Dream Coat*!
But it was meaningful work and enjoyable learning. We produced
the Bible Pageant at the school open night and the local Baptist
minister asked us to do it in his church one evening. I had not
wanted to go into teaching, but when I did I realised how valuable
a training it was for what I was destined to do next.

I had not been teaching for long, when one day the
telephone rang at home. It was the Moderator of the United Free
Church, who was scheduled to visit the UF church in Burntisland
one Sunday in February. He asked if I would be willing to take the
service in his own church in Leith on that day. I said I would be
pleased to. He knew my situation and said how sorry he was that
I had not been able to be a minister, and if he could help he would.
I thanked him.

On the Sunday in question, a neighbouring minister arrived
before the service to tell us that the Moderator had died suddenly
the night before at Burntisland church manse. The news was
broken to the congregation and I went into the pulpit to conduct
the service that morning. The people obviously loved their
minister: some were very upset and were being comforted by
others. I had prepared carefully, helped by my teacher training, but
as the service proceeded, I felt I must scrap my preparation and
speak as God guided me in this situation. So I knelt in the pulpit
and prayed for God to help me. The congregation told me (and

have repeated for years after), 'You were sent to us that day. Will you come and be our minister?' Here was the Call, if ever there was one. Here was the open door when all the others had been closed.

Elliot and I prayed for guidance and spoke to old and wise friends, including our minister, Revd Martin Shields, and Revd Charles Smith (then Principal Clerk of the Edinburgh Presbytery). He had been the chaplain to Boroughmuir School when I was head girl and he had taken a great interest in my future. Elliot and I were assured this was God's will for both of us, and the congregation of Hermitage United Free Church, Leith, was also sure.

It was a wrench leaving St. Ninian's, but Elliot and I found we could agree to the tenets of the United Free Church and so we joined Corstorphine UF Church.

In 1930 the General Assembly of the United Free Church of Scotland had passed a resolution that any member in full communion was eligible to hold any office in the church. In this way it recognised its laypeople, but it also opened the door for women to be ordained to the eldership, and to the ministry.

Revd Elizabeth B. Barr MA BD was ordained and inducted in 1935 to Auchterarder United Free Church. She was appointed Moderator of the General Assembly of the United Free Church in 1960. 'It was an amazing honour,' she told us, 'not because I was a woman, but because I was the woman I was.' She liked to think that the General Assembly was honouring the women of the church and yet she held to her belief that men and women are one in Christ. Through Christ we have received the at-one-ment with God.

My call was tested by the United Free Church Presbytery of Edinburgh and I was accepted by the Assembly as a candidate for the ministry. I completed my trials and was licensed by the Presbytery, called by Hermitage United Free Church to be their minister and ordained and inducted on October 7 1955. So I began a long ministry of service in the old port of Leith – a community of docks and shipyards; of tenements and bustling shops; of proud traditions, plain speaking and warm hearts.

In the first week of my ministry I was asked by a member to visit her neighbour, who was in a nursing home in town. I set out

one morning feeling very uncertain: I had never met the lady and
I did not know the nursing home. As chance would have it, I met
my mother up town, and told her where I was going. 'Well, it was
your choice to be a minister and you'll just have to get on with it,'
she said. This was not the way my mother usually spoke to me. She
normally sympathised and encouraged me, but I think she was
right to spur me on, although I didn't like it one little bit! I found
the nursing home, met Matron, and explained who I was and that
I had been sent to visit the lady. She conducted me along darkly lit
corridors and into a gloomy room. She introduced me to the patient
and left me. What a shock I got when my eyes got used to the light
and I saw the gaunt patient – a kind of copper colour, dreadfully
ill, dying. With God's help I ministered to her, with Bible readings
and prayers commending her to God's love, forgiveness and eternal
blessings. I came out shaken and with difficulty got home. The
telephone rang – it was the member of my congregation who had
sent me on the visit. The old lady had just died. Nothing prepares
you for such experiences but God sees you through and you are
His handmaid.

I threw myself into the church work and loved it, but after
several months I became very ill: so ill that I had to go to hospital
for several weeks. When I learned that my first baby was coming,
and that, despite the trouble, all was well, I wrote to the Session
offering to resign. They met and I received a letter from the Session
Clerk, Mr John Landels: 'When the congregation called you to be
their minister they knew you were a young married woman. They
had already discussed the probability of your having a family. They
hoped you would. Now that you are going to, please do not leave
us. We rejoice with you and your husband and pray for your
speedy return to health.' Once again my ministry had been
confirmed. How different from these modern days when a minister
intimated from the pulpit one Sunday that she was pregnant and
the congregation applauded! How different now that there is
maternity and paternity leave too.

The gift of our first son Elliot was indeed a great blessing, not
only to us, but to the whole congregation. We have four sons and

all were welcomed and took their place in the church family. When the babies were coming I was able to continue the pastoral work, the visitations, the funerals, the baptisms, weddings, meetings and most services. The congregation was faithful and loyal, and expressed appreciation of the ministers who gave pulpit supply when I was unable to preach. Apart from these times and a few operations, I have not been off duty in all the years of my ministry. I have never neglected my family, nor have I neglected my congregation. I have found one to be the complement of the other and in loving and serving both, I find relief, fulfilment and joy.

My ministry involved taking meetings of the Board, the Session and even the Presbytery, of which I became Moderator. A Moderator moderates: it is not I, but Christ who rules in me. The pastoral work I did conscientiously, visiting my people, and I was accepted by young and old, by male and female. My approach to work was a personal one. I made no pretensions to being a man either in my dress or my behaviour, or by doing my job in a 'manly' way. I offered the comfort of God to the sufferer. I offered my own experience if I had it to others. I took the services every Sunday and prepared, as my teaching and pastoral training had disciplined me to do. My aim was and is always to bring everyone into God's presence so that we may worship Him together. I took baptisms and helped the young parents to see what a wonderful gift they had been given; how precious this life was and how important to bring their child up in God's way. The Bible Class and the Youth Fellowship loved to ask questions and debate, and I loved to tussle with them on the issues of the day. I found my training had all been part of God's wonderful way of preparing me for the ministry. A newspaper commentator wrote, 'The harrowing experience of a graveside is not for any woman.' I have seen death in the young and the old. I have seen death as a lovely and blessed thing but I have also seen it in all its horror and pain. Always I have sought to bring the comfort of Jesus Christ to the sufferer. I remind them of the love of one who knew pain and torment on the Cross. Never have I conducted a funeral that has been a 'harrowing experience'.

There has been sorrow, deep sorrow, and the minister enters into that sorrow. But ours is the Gospel of the Son of God – the Man of Sorrows who loves us each one so much that He gave his life for us. He conquered death, rose victorious over the grave and promises eternal life to all who follow him and put their trust in him.

On my first visit as a minister to the Royal Infirmary I walked through the big glass doors of the ward where a member of my congregation was. Before me stood a tall, formidable-looking sister with arms crossed over her big chest. I approached and addressed her politely: 'Sister, please could I see Mrs A who is a member of my congregation?' Sister drew herself up and towered above me even more. 'Is she a relative of yours?' 'No Sister,' I replied 'she is one of my congregation. I am her minister.' From her height she looked down at me with great distaste. 'Sit outside on the bench there. You're too early.' On my way through the door another minister passed me – a man. 'Oh good day, Mr A,' said the Sister. 'You'll find Mrs T much better.' Off he went to see his member. A third minister came in while I sat on the bench. 'Come away in, Mr W,' said Sister, blithely greeting him and accompanying him into the ward. I plucked up courage and joined another group going in. As I passed, Sister looked down. 'Yes, you may come in now,' she said rather condescendingly.

In contrast, one of my male elders was in hospital. He had been a widower for some time. He was an inspector of ships whose job was to make sure that they were seaworthy. Most of his life he had worked with men at shipyards, and I hoped he would not be embarrassed by my visiting him since I was heavily pregnant. I reached the door of the ward and he saw me and said in his usual loud and clear voice, 'Oh Sister, here's my minister I was telling you about. Come and meet her.' She dropped everything and came to be introduced. What a happy time I had. We visited and he introduced me to everyone in the ward with the same enthusiasm as he had announced my entry. Before I left, Sister and some of the men gathered round his bed for Bible reading and prayers, conducted by me.

The same man had to have a toe amputated. The specialist feared his foot would have to go too. The doctors met to discuss his case, and decided to delay the decision for a weekend. We heard the serious news. We prayed in private. We prayed in public at our Sunday Service: 'If it is your will, God, bring healing to our elder and friend.' On Monday when the bandages came off there were signs of healing in the toe and the foot was saved. The doctors and staff said it was a miracle.

There has been great controversy over the years regarding women in the ministry: sociological, physiological, biological, practical arguments and a whole weight of tradition have been brought to bear on this subject. The debate was certainly raging in the churches, especially in the Church of Scotland, during the early years of my ministry.

I cannot tell you how painful it was to find such animosity and unwillingness to listen to women who tried to explain why they thought God had called them in the same way as He had called men. In the first twelve years of my ministry I felt I was being watched by others to prove that women could be ministers, could be married ministers and mothers; that women were able – no matter how strenuous, emotionally draining and pressurised the ministry was. I felt the best way to prove anything was to be the person God made me. I was indeed blessed by a most loving, helpful husband. I had parents, relatives and friends who were willing to child-mind and also help in any situation. The church officer-bearers were very conscientious in their office, and the congregation was united in God's love and service. As for my own calling, Paul was and is my example. Whenever Paul's apostleship was questioned, he replied by recalling how God had called him on the Damascus Road. My own story, which I share here, is the answer I give to those who question my vocation. As Paul defends himself as an apostle, so do I as a minister, chosen, called by God and given God's help to be a steward in his service.

By 1963 the Church of Scotland had moved a little by

licensing women to preach, but the debate about women in the ministry rumbled on. Since my call out of the Church of Scotland, I felt my part was to speak at all the meetings on the subject up and down the country. Wherever I was invited, I told how God had called me and equipped me for His service.

Other women ministers did likewise, but the Church of Scotland had to be petitioned again. In May 1963 God raised up a tall, dignified, very intelligent, spiritually gifted young lady for this specific task. Mary Lusk MA, BD, DCS, who had already been licensed to preach, petitioned the General Assembly that she might be ordained as a minister of the church. 'This time the Fathers and Brethren listened, deeply moved, to the appeal of this so obviously dedicated and gifted young woman,' wrote dear Revd D.P. Thomson, the Church of Scotland evangelist.

The Assembly referred Miss Lusk's petition and the whole issue of women in the ministry to the Panel on Doctrine. It was to be five more years before the Church of Scotland ordained women.

I attended three Kirk Weeks, in Aberdeen, Dundee and Ayr and to the last two the family also came – an innovation in these days. Over the years I was a member of many committees: the Kirk Week Council, the Edinburgh Ecumenical Association Committee, the 'Tell Scotland' Committee, and the Multilateral Conversations, the BBC Religious Broadcasting Advisory Committee and the Local Churches Religious Broadcasting Committee. I served on all of these, and others too, and enjoyed the fellowship of representatives from other denominations and churches. I organised a special Children's Service in Princes Street Gardens one summer and part of this was televised in a Songs of Praise Service. Such activities brought us all closer together.

Through the years my ministry has changed in order to serve the community better. There was a shortage of nursery places in Leith, so we decided to open up the church building for a playschool. I was able to run this because I had my teacher's certificate. How far-seeing God is! It was a wonderful experience to watch the children inside and outside in the garden enjoying themselves. When a train passed by on the other side of the wall, the drivers always stopped to wave to them and the children waved back. It was a boon having parents and friends from the neighbourhood who came and helped at the playschool. We all learned so much from each other. We had happy pageants and pantomimes, with all the children taking part, while the grown-ups made the scenery and costumes. The whole experience of the playschool brought out the best in each of us. We shared fun, sympathy and real caring – for each other, for the children and for the community too. The playschool ran for twelve years, by which time there was new provision in the schools for nursery children, and so we felt our time for meeting this need had come to an end.

More pressing problems had arisen – unemployment and substandard housing for too many people. The Leith Community Association elected me as chairperson, and with the help of many others we ran government schemes for the unemployed. We conducted surveys to discover how people lived – especially the elderly. These highlighted the need for help with gardens and cleaning; for better insulation; and for lighting in streets and stairs. We had a FISH Scheme to try to make people aware of their neighbours: how they might befriend them in cold weather or, if they were getting old, just to make sure they were all right each day. Each household had a fish which they could place in their window if they needed help. These initiatives encouraged a building up of the community.

People asked me, 'Why don't you stand for the Council?' I thought that might be a way to meet the needs of folk in the community, so I asked my congregation what they thought. They supported me, and I stood as a candidate at a by-election. Despite being 'a local community volunteer, non-party candidate', I got a respectable vote but came third. At the next Council election I improved my vote. However, I could see I would never be elected without a party.

In 1982, I became one of the religious representatives on the Education Committee for Lothian Region, and I was later approached by two friends I respected greatly – one a Democrat, the other a Liberal. (These political parties later formed the Liberal Democrats.) They asked me to stand in the next Edinburgh District election. I agreed and was elected, after a recount, by nineteen votes! That night there was a landslide vote for a Labour Council. I had taken the only Labour seat which was lost and some held that against me. However, I have worked hard to serve my Leith constituents and the Council for the past fifteen years.

The Leith Council of Churches has continued growing together in united services, in sharing our celebrations with others and publicly proclaiming we are one in Christ. We have built bridges with the Pakistanis in our midst, welcoming and being welcomed by them, and similarly with other groups from other lands.

I was a United Free Church representative on the Multilateral Conversations. We all conscientiously studied our divisions and tried to find reasons and ways to overcome them. Once again we all suffered the pain of separation and disunity, yet the very effort of trying to overcome barriers was so difficult. One positive outcome was the individual friendships that we made and the one great success was when we were able to agree on our Christian Baptism. A baptismal card was produced, which many of the churches agreed to accept. In all my ecumenical activities and contacts, I discovered that what bound us together, and helped break through the barriers, was that through Christ we were learning to accept one another.

As we move into the millennium, preparing ourselves with years of Faith and Hope, I pray that we move to a real and faithful global witness of the basic truth expressed in a popular song, that 'They will know we are Christians by our Love'.

Leith Community Association, working alongside other organisations such as the YMCA, developed several initiatives to meet some of the greatest needs within our community. We started projects for the unemployed and to help the elderly, who were checked daily. The first Lunch Club, which started in Leith, spread elsewhere. We had a Lunch Club in our church, which led to the establishment of a government community programme for the elderly: especially those discharged from hospital, who were visited by our YMCA-trained team. One day a week they helped to bring these elderly folk to the church hall for afternoon tea and entertainment – all produced by the team. We hired a bus and volunteer neighbours drove them home. This supported many vulnerable elderly folk, and was much commended by the doctors, ministers and all involved. Alas, the government stopped the funding and within a fortnight the scheme had closed. The day we announced this the old folks wept and said to the team, 'Oh dear, we will miss you. You will be losing your jobs! That's terrible.' And the team comforted them, saying, 'Don't worry about us. We'll manage. Just take good care of yourselves.'

As we looked on we had such mixed feelings: anger that a government should stop a scheme without more warning; yet so proud of the team, who cared more for the old folk than for themselves; and moved by the dear souls in their concern about the young ones.

For twenty-six years the community fought for a new building to replace the old Leith Academy. When the beautiful modern school was built the congregation was contacted and asked if we would sell our church and grounds for a suitable pedestrian entry to the school from another main road. We agreed – provided that the remaining area of our ground and of the old school buildings would be used for purpose-designed sheltered housing. So Hermitage Court, with fifty sheltered homes, was constructed, and Hermitage Church congregation moved into the school for worship.

As a Councillor I find a bigger outreach to many non-church folks whom I am privileged to serve, and I continue all my work as a woman in the ministry.

When my husband suffered a very bad heart attack and was in the intensive care unit in hospital, the church folk in Leith (of all denominations) prayed for him. He was granted the miracle of five more very active years: doing beautiful calligraphy and playing music for Leith Festivals, and sharing these gifts for the enjoyment of many people. When he died, I received prayer cards and letters from ministers, Roman Catholic priests, and members of all the local churches, who also attended his funeral service of thanksgiving.

In 1972, I attended a meeting in the Church of Scotland's Assembly Hall. There I shared in the wonderful experience of being led in prayer by Dr George MacLeod, founder of the Iona Community. I came home and wrote down the vision God gave me that day:

I Have a Dream for Leith

I have a dream for Leith
a dream where there are pleasant homes and happy people.
They have work to do and are content.

I have a dream for the Church in Leith
which belongs to God in His service,
to serve the people of Leith,
to act as leaven in the community,
to broaden their vision
and bring in those whom God is calling.

To hear the cry of people far and near for comfort, help,
understanding, sympathy, justice and freedom.
To answer that cry sacrificially and in the love of God.

I have a dream that from this dispirited, disillusioned,
depressed area
there will arise
a community which shines with the light of God upon its life
enfolding within it – the stranger from other lands,
the homeless, the refugee,
the visitor in port,
the vigorous young and the honoured old.
A place where God is
and where all bear God's mark of love.

4　... *And set my feet upon a Rock*[1]

Margaret Forrester

What makes a person move from a conventional pattern to a more unusual course? What motivates a person to engage with the pain involved in change? Genes? Upbringing? External factors? I find it difficult even now, with sixty years of hindsight, to interpret events in my life in any other way except in terms of vocation.

Born on the eve of the second world war, the second daughter of a comfortable professional family in Edinburgh, my earliest memories were of war-time and of the importance and fragility of family life. We were together for only one weekend per month and I realised then and now that we were luckier than many. Most of all I was aware of the centrality of God and the church in my parents' life. My father, son of a Highland manse, was a kirk elder from his student days in Edinburgh. He was a chartered accountant and treasurer of West St Giles for thirty-two years. My present to him on his birthday when I was only four was to learn and recite to him Psalm 100 from the Scottish Metrical Psalter. This nauseatingly pious confession was neither as nauseating nor as pious as it sounds. No one spent money on presents in war-time. My mother, a teacher by profession and instinct, loved teaching us – poems, ballads, songs. I loved learning things. My father loved the psalms. After the recitation, the party moved on to scones and cake made with powdered egg, to telling stories, singing songs and dancing around the piano while my mother played. She came, via a Devonshire childhood, from Skye and could sing in Gaelic. Although she competed in the Mod, both in choirs and as a soloist, she never took her considerable musical talents seriously. 'With your Grandpa spending the first ten years of my life in the dockyards at Devonport, I never developed the real "miaouw" for the Mod singing!' she used to say.

In spite of the shadow of war, life was secure. I do not suppose for one minute that my parents never argued – but my sister and I were never aware of it, and all the evidence points to a twelve-year marriage of remarkable contentment, in spite of the age difference of nineteen years. Only once, in August 1945, when the long-awaited journey to and holiday in the Highlands took place and we spent a sun-drenched month in Invergordon – did the sun really shine almost every day that summer? – was I aware of a tension, a frisson, between them. My mother's strong, robust voice saying, as I came into the room, 'What else was there to do, Willie? We have to end things now.' And my father's softer voice saying, 'But Mary, not twice. Not two so soon. We don't know enough.' And then the 'not-in-front-of-the-children' look came down over both their faces, and they asked bland, benign questions about beaches and sea shells and sand castles. I felt excluded from a more interesting and dangerously divisive adult conversation. It was many years before I realised that I had almost taken part in my first discussion about nuclear weapons.

That year, 1945–1946 was a strange one in our family. Two years previously we had returned to Edinburgh after four years in the country. My sister and I were sent to a fee-paying girls' school. I missed the village school and my country friends. I was slow to adapt to the noises and smells and oppressive ways of city life. The acquisition of a kitten was an attempt by our parents to compensate for the loss of the wide open spaces and started my lifelong enjoyment of cats. My father, who had had polio as a toddler and walked supported by heavy iron callipers and with the aid of two sticks, became mysteriously forced to rest. He still went to the office, but rested when he came home, rested on Saturdays and, most amazing of all, rested on Sunday evenings, thereby missing the evening service. My mother and sister, Anne, felt that one service on a Sunday was enough. But I genuinely loved church, and along with Gretta, our young housekeeper, friend and confidante, would cheerfully go by tram to West St Giles and sit with a warm and friendly congregation through a service that was both incomprehensible and yet amazingly inclusive and welcoming. Sitting in that dimly lit church I would listen to a sermon so opaque that I could carry little back to my father except the text, and not always that. What unbelievably I *did* carry back was his Gladstone bag with the offering envelopes inside. Others counted the cash, but the envelopes were opened by no one else but my father.

That year, in spite of the adventure of the Highland holiday, was a twilight year. Not for a moment did Anne and I think that the effort to get there might be to say farewell to the relations and friends in the north. Nor did we consider that the enforced resting was because our father was ill. Even when he had a severe stroke in March 1946, and was taken to a nursing home, we were shielded by well-intentioned adults and never suspected that we should not see him again. And when, exactly one week later, he died, we were both totally stunned.

What a brutal emotional discipline descended. Is it Scottish? Is it cultural? Is it Calvinist? Was it the fashion at the time? Was it part of a war-fatigued community that accepted sudden death as commonplace? Was it just our family? I do not know. I do know that we were not expected to cry or show any sign of distress – 'It will upset your mother.' Presumably she was told by the same well-meaning relatives not to cry because 'it will upset the children'. We were allowed off school for one day and then went back. We were not allowed to go to the funeral. And when, a few weeks later, I asked my best friend (up from the country to stay with me for Easter) if she knew that my father had died, she held my hand and said, 'Yes, but we'll not talk about it.' One year later, when a beautiful stained glass memorial window designed by William Wilson was unveiled and we had just sung my father's favourite hymn, one undisciplined tear began to drip down my cheek. Gretta, normally so kind and sympathetic, looked down at me and whispered sternly, 'Don't you start.' So I didn't.

And so we settled down to an all-female household – my mother, a teacher in a private senior school in Edinburgh, Gretta the housekeeper, my sister Anne and I. It was a privileged upbringing by most standards, but it was also narrow and inhibiting. There were no men in the immediate family and I find myself able to empathise with the young girl in *The Lady's Not for Burning* who confesses that men were an unknown quantity, and that it was a surprise to her that they spoke English! Our social circle was not so much small as non-existent. In those days, women who went out to work were looked at askance, especially when they did not have to do it for financial reasons. With hindsight, I realise how unconventional my mother was, as indeed was my father who had always encouraged her to do what she loved to do, teach. At the time, I just found it all very embarrassing in that middle class milieu to have a mother who was different. I also gradually came to understand how lonely she was. Widowhood was not easily absorbed into the culture of the forties and fifties.

She died of cancer in my first year at New College and only during those last months was I able to ask her about her life, her dreams, her grief. With some ancestral Free Kirk shadow hovering around her and gripping her as tightly as the cancer, she believed that God was punishing her for past misdeeds. I can remember then crying with her and trying to convince her that God was gracious and of unending kindness. But even in her last illness, her biblical knowledge was superior to mine, and she produced text after text from the OT of judgement and guilt and punishment.

I wanted to call out the woman who had taught me how to country dance, how to make oatcakes, how to turn the heel of a sock, how to read Dickens and Scott, how to like whodunits and crosswords, who had shared her love of music and oratorio and opera, who had taught me how to play bridge and do algebra and to enjoy living. But although she believed she was among the Elect, the cancer had to be accepted as punishment for sin. Although I have often since sat by the bed of a dying person, I have never again felt such a weight of anguish.

Within the year of my father's death, I heard a missionary home on furlough speak at Sunday School. I came home and announced that God wanted me to be a missionary. It goes without saying that such a decision at such a time by so young and vulnerable a child was ridiculous. All I can say is that, firstly, I was aware of the presence of God and had a love for the church long before the death of my father. Secondly, my mother treated what I said with an open seriousness which pressurised me neither into following nor abandoning that call. And thirdly, the sense of call has lasted.

At the same time, I learned from both my mother and Sunday School teachers that 'girls can't be ministers' – a fact of life which I accepted without question. And from the same sources, I learned that 'women could be teachers, doctors or nurses'. There were too many teachers in our family and a doctor appeared to me to be more useful in an African setting – and possibly more romantic! The *Jungle Doctor* books had a big impact on me at that time. Thus for the next nine or ten years, I settled down happily enough to life at school, church and home, hugely influenced by the Scripture Union branch at school and enjoying the publication of the then Foreign Mission Committee, *Other Lands*. In that television-less society, I devoured books and haunted Morningside public library. On one occasion during the school holidays, having read the three books which I had taken out in the morning, I tried to return them the same afternoon. The poor harassed librarian leant over the counter and said, 'Go away until tomorrow!' I made good friends at school, enjoyed Guides at church, went to Sunday School and Bible Class and attended evening service of my own free will – unusual even then. At the age of sixteen, along with thirty or so other young people, I 'joined the church'.

The only blip that appeared on a fairly clear horizon at that time was that my study of science at school appeared to indicate that the Darwinian theory of evolution was true. On the other hand, my Scripture Union mentors felt that it was an article of faith to believe in a six-day creation. It was presented as a test of orthodoxy. Without having the words or the theology to discuss the issue, I paid lip service to conservative theory but privately clung to the liberating words of Jesus: 'You will know the truth and the truth will make you free.'[2] As Jesus himself was and is the truth, seekers of truth have no need to fear or to hide behind spurious arguments. I decided quite carefully that, within God's world, what science taught and what Genesis Chapter 1 recorded could probably be held together comfortably. They could lie side by side, both containing truth, neither of them defining to the point of excluding the other, and both pointing to the glory of God's creating.

In my first year of studies at the University of Edinburgh, after ten years of moving fairly effortlessly towards the goal of becoming a medical missionary, I came up against an obstacle. Not only did I find the academic work difficult, I found it and the entire ethos inimical. That I had to work hard to keep up would have been no problem in itself. The fact that I felt so out of place, so abandoned, so lost, was something I found very difficult to cope with. For the first time in my life, I had to analyse what was happening. Up until then, I had accepted everything that had happened to me as ordered, pre-ordained, to be accepted dutifully, obediently and unquestioningly. Now, for the first time, I had to think what I was doing, what God was doing.

It may seem strange in the closing years of this century that any young woman could so easily acquiesce in the role laid down for her by society. But this was in the 1950s. It was before the university riots in Paris or the Kent State University student demonstrations in the USA. It was before Betty Friedan's *The Feminine Mystique* or Germaine Greer's *The Female Eunuch*. It was before liberation theology and the feminist movement. It was not a questing or questioning time. It was accepted that men home from the war should have advantaged places at university and in employment. It was accepted that certain jobs were not open to women or open only in a partial and limited way. In the Faculties of Medicine, Dentistry and Veterinary Medicine, places for women were limited to under twenty per cent. At the time it seemed like a lot less.

Now, I had to ask what God was doing in my own situation. For it never occurred to me that God was not in this. Everything I had read in the Bible, everything that I had been taught at home and church and school made me quite sure that whatever the confusion it was not God's. For the first time I looked at the possibility that the call I had received at the age of eight might have been too narrowly interpreted. For the first time I recalled that my careers teacher at school had looked at my exam results when I was fourteen or fifteen as I was making a final selection of subjects to take for Highers and had said to me, 'What a pity you are not a boy. You are not very good at science, but with your strength in English and Latin and your interest in the church, you should be thinking of being a minister. But, of course, you can't.' Of course.

What finally forced me to think of something other than medical missions was a remarkably fine day conference held in the Chaplaincy Centre at the University of Edinburgh and organised by the then chaplain, Revd James Blackie, on the theme 'Full Time Work in the Church'. At that conference as a principal speaker was Mary Lusk. For the first time in my life I engaged in real theological debate about myself. I could have chattered away for hours about atonement and predestination, but to question *myself* theologically was new. For the first time I saw that God continued to call and lead and prod. For the first time I felt that ambiguities and questions and anomalies and tentativeness were part of obedience. I had to grasp the idea that I was being headed away from medicine towards something less secure, less ordered, less prestigious, with no promise and absolutely no certainty. For the first time I had to abandon my own reasoned thinking and felt that I had to take a risk in God's name.

In the 1950s when a teenage girl announced that she was going to be a medical missionary, the response was usually one of awed admiration, certainly of approval. We were still in the aftermath of the Tell Scotland Campaign and the Billy Graham All Scotland Crusade. To indicate, however tentatively, that I thought I might be called to the ministry of the church elicited very different responses. 'Are you telling the church that it is wrong?' 'Do you think you know better than God?' 'Are you saying that the church has been wrong for two thousand years?' 'What makes you so special?' 'Do you think God would choose someone like you?' 'Have you never read the Bible?'

Perhaps wisely, I decided that time would test the call and I settled into an enjoyable time in the Faculty of Arts where I discovered the delights of the Student Christian Movement. Invigorating Bible studies, sturdy theological discussion, ecumenical awareness and companionable friendships took up most of my time. I was breaking out of the prison house of a faith and a theology that had become too small. Or rather I was introduced to a theology that allowed, indeed compelled, questioning and discussion and seeking. The text that I had clung to as a youngster took on a new lustre: 'You will know the truth, and the truth will make you free.'[3] To love God with one's mind demanded not only obedience, but intellectual rigour.

Towards the end of Session 1960–61, I applied to be a student at the Faculty of Divinity and with reluctance applied to be trained as a deaconess of the Church of Scotland. The former turned out to be easy, even when I insisted on taking the entrance exams required for New College, exams that had to be passed by those who were candidates for the ministry. The Scottish university system is such that the Faculty of Divinity of the university is also the church seminary. Most students came to take the BD degree, at that time always a second degree, after graduating in arts or science, and at the same time to train for the ministry. It was possible to take a degree in theology and ignore the extra courses and training required by the church. I was determined to do everything that the church required as well as a degree in theology.

It is difficult to convey now the diffidence with which a woman would enter such a male bastion. Women had taken degrees in theology before – Elizabeth Hewat and Mary Lusk to name the two best known. But to start from day one with the avowed intention of asking the church to reconsider its position demanded a degree of confidence and pertinacity which I did not believe I had.

I have said that I was reluctant to apply to become a deaconess. This was not in any way because the diaconate was a calling or profession I disliked. By now, my vocation was focused on ministry, unattainable and unlikely though it appeared to be, and it seemed dishonest to seek to join that hospitable group of women, the deaconesses of the Church of Scotland, when I felt so strongly that I had been called to ministry. It worried me that I might appear to be using them to my own ends. But I tried to remain obedient to the church and the only office open to women at the time was the office of deaconess. So in September 1961 I started as a boarder at St Colm's College where deaconesses and missionaries were trained and the following month began the degree course at New College. St Colm's had a fine group of staff – Jean Fraser, Mary Lusk, Kenneth Mackenzie, to name only a few – and I did my best to fit in. But most of my waking hours were spent at New College. The Faculty of Arts had been good, but theology was my métier. That year, dominated as it was by visits to my very sick mother (she died in the July), was yet overwhelmingly happy as I knew beyond any shadow of doubt that I had found my home – both intellectual and spiritual – in New College.

Some members of staff were deeply and sympathetically supportive, notably Robin Barbour, James Stewart, Norman Porteous and George Anderson, but at that time opposition to the ordination of women existed and was open. Those who opposed were vocal and organised. Some used biblical arguments. Texts were lifted neatly out of cultural or religious context and presented as permanent or absolute truths. For example, there were those who would quote, 'I permit no woman to teach'.[4] Taking that out of context and applying it literally would close down almost every Sunday School in the country, not to mention day schools. Sometimes the earlier account of creation in Genesis 2 was presented as the inalienable order of creation. Any attempt to set against this the four gospel accounts of women as the first witnesses of the resurrection was met with amazement. The resurrection command 'Go quickly and tell his disciples that he has been raised from the dead . . .'[5] has always been for me the reality of the New Covenant. The precious news of the resurrection was entrusted to women.

Some were opposed on grounds of tradition. 'It has never been . . .' was the cry. 'There were no women among the disciples,' said some. Nor were there non-Jews, or Africans, or Indians, or white Anglo-Saxon males.

Some felt that ecumenical relationships would be jeopardised. But this tended to be an argument put forward by those who did not want to disturb a good relationship with the Church of England. Those who argued in this way paid scant attention to what our brothers and sisters in the World Alliance of Reformed Churches were doing, or the Congregationalists, or the Methodists or the Lutherans. And if I or others suggested that this was a movement from God which would eventually embrace the Anglicans and even the Church of Rome, we were laughed to scorn.

It was almost enjoyable to take on allcomers at this reasonable level of debate.

Other arguments were downright emotional and insulting. 'Women's brains can't cope with Hebrew.' This gem was offered seriously by a nervous Anglican at a conference of the Student Christian Movement. 'Women don't have powerful enough voices.' This came from a student at New College. *All* the arguments had an element of emotion and fear and jealousy as people felt that cherished traditions were being threatened. I have seen it since in many areas of debate, and I constantly have to ask myself whether any gut response I may have to anything new or different is based on more than prejudice.

In 1963, Mary Lusk, by this time Assistant Chaplain of Edinburgh University, petitioned the General Assembly and asked the Church of Scotland to test her call. Her own account of these times may be read in her book, *Wrestling with the Church*. It would be impossible to underestimate the debt all women ministers in the Church of Scotland owe to Mary Lusk, now Dr Mary Levison. Her academic record, her remarkable years of service, her quiet dignity in leadership have been an inspiration. I was one of the throng of students who packed out the gallery of the Assembly Hall in 1963. The atmosphere in the Hall was electric, both sides aware that history was in the making. The petition was gracious, cogent and incisive. The level of debate was high, and that gentle Moderator, James S. Stewart, himself an ardent supporter of the ordination of women, had to rebuke the students in the gallery on several occasions for the applause that broke out. Four years after that, I was one of the six theologically trained women who wrote 'An Open Letter to the General Assembly of the Church of Scotland', which was released at a press conference following the report of the Panel on Doctrine and prior to the debate at the Assembly. But I am anticipating.

Events in my own life were moving swiftly. The following year, in April 1964, I was commissioned as a deaconess of the Church of Scotland with licence to preach. Within two weeks I became engaged to Duncan Forrester, a missionary teacher home on leave from India, sat my final exams, and was married in St George's West church. The following month I graduated BD, specialising in New Testament Literature and Language. A few weeks later I joined my husband in Madras Christian College, South India, where Duncan, a presbyter of the Church of South India, taught politics. There, while acclimatising to a tropical climate, marriage and campus life, I taught a diploma course in OT theology and started a class in NT Greek for those who intended to proceed to theological college. Teaching was a new experience and of course I was totally untrained, but I found it hugely enjoyable. Best of all, I became pastoral assistant to the presbyter in Tambaram, Revd R.T. Bhaskeran, now Bishop of Vellore. I had special responsibility for the English-speaking part of his large pastorate. Four years and two children later, in 1968, the Act was passed admitting women to the ministry on the same terms and conditions as those applicable to men. My mother-in-law, Isobel Forrester, an ardent supporter of women ministers and a great encourager, sent a cable to us in India. It read: 'Sweeping victory for the ordination of women.' I still have it, framed, in my study.

Although we left India in 1970, my husband's work took him to England and it was the hospitable United Reformed Church in its exciting and challenging infancy which ordained me on 23rd January 1974, when I was called to the small pastorate in Telscombe Cliffs, Sussex. One of the hymns I chose for the ordination service was Psalm 40 from the Scottish Metrical Psalter. The title of this chapter is a quote from that psalm. For many years, most of my life, I had been aware of an overpowering sense of vocation which every church in which I worshipped had refused to recognise. The frustration and pain of this were hard to bear. It did now appear that after the fearful pits and the miry clay, my feet were set upon a rock.

We returned to Scotland in 1978, when Duncan became Professor of Christian Ethics and Practical Theology at New College, Edinburgh. Shortly after, I was asked by Revd Dr Bill Cattanach of St George's West to be his assistant minister and enjoyed his invigorating preaching and generous colleagueship. In 1980 St Michael's church became vacant and in the same year I was called to be their minister on the basis of terminable tenure, at the same time to develop the new chaplaincy in Napier College as part-time chaplain for three years. After three years, it was decided to have a full-time chaplain at Napier, and St Michael's was restored to full status.

The years at St Michael's have been full of learning and growing and pain and fulfilment for me both as a person and as a minister. Before my Introduction, one of the Vacancy Committee told me that they had not wanted a woman minister and had only chosen me because 'being made terminable by Presbytery, we were scraping the bottom of the barrel'. He went on to observe gloomily that I had been 'the best of a bad bunch'. These things were said in jest. I hope that no elder now would think of saying such a thing to any minister.

It is difficult to convey in a few words the sense of excitement and adventure I find in my work as a parish minister. To spend nearly eighteen years with one congregation means that one cannot run away from mistakes. One becomes part of the community, sharing grief and joy, learning of one's own inadequacies and accepting the awesome responsibility of weekly preaching. I know that the friendship and forgiveness of my congregation and their prayers and generosity enfold me and sustain me. Much of what I know of ministry they have taught me.

Being married to a minister who is an academic means that I

have a constant source of theological stimulation. But an unlooked-for support came from our children. Our son Donald from an early age questioned my theology and was ruthless in exposing sloppy thinking or inconsistencies in practice. Catriona, equally passionate about justice, was more involved in the life of the church, and any success that there has been in youth work in St Michael's church I owe largely to her generosity of time and skill. Her musical ability and imaginative art work made successive years of holiday clubs memorable for many children. Both Donald and Catriona are now social workers, in London and Paisley respectively.

And now, thirty years after the Act was passed in 1968, what is the position of ordained women in the Church of Scotland?

Undoubtedly there is still opposition. But it is more clandestine, more oblique, less provable and more self-deluded than before. It is comparatively easy for a woman to get a charge – a first charge. So rural and isolated areas, terminable charges, assistantships, run-down inner city charges, urban priority charges are there for any hard-working woman. They may move to a second 'first charge' but the so-called 'second charge' is still beyond the reach of most women ministers. By 'second charge' I refer to the comfortable suburban charges, largely professional in make-up with no financial problems and with good lay leadership, or the prosperous city centre charges or the large county town churches. The very recent and richly deserved appointment of Revd Susan Brown to Dornoch Cathedral is the first break-through in this area. I have particular delight in this appointment as she spent the second year of her Diploma in Ministry with me in St Michael's. The Revd Jean Montgomerie was Convener of the Board of Ministry and I was Convener of the Board of World Mission. But the proportion of ordained women being offered leadership roles in the church is not high.

There has been speculation for some years now about the nomination of the first woman Moderator of the General Assembly. Each autumn the press makes life difficult for senior women ministers as names are bandied about often with no basis in fact and in spite of the truthful denial of the woman concerned. To my

certain knowledge, three women so far have been approached and
have allowed their names to go forward. None so far has been
nominated. Is this the glass ceiling which women experience in
other professions? I leave it to others to judge. It would appear that
the representatives of Presbyteries and the former Moderators who
make up the nomination committee are determined to be safe
rather than to take such a risk for what is after all only a one-year
terminable appointment! Although the Scottish Episcopal Church
was some twenty-five years behind the Church of Scotland in
ordaining women, perhaps they may consecrate the first bishop
before the Presbyterians have a woman Moderator.

That women are coming into ministry in increasing numbers
is very clear. I hope that they will enjoy the satisfaction and fulfilment in ministry that I have, and experience a universally
supportive and equal colleagueship with all other ministers. It is
now thirty-five years since I was licensed to preach, and now
twenty-five since I was ordained. It is difficult to convey the
enormous change that has taken place in the Church of Scotland
during that time. I hope that I have managed to convey something
of the sense of privilege and joy that I have felt in being part of this
time of change and renewal in the church.

Notes and references

1   Metrical Psalm 40:2

2   John 8:32

3   ibid.

4   1 Timothy 2:12

5   Matthew 28:7

5   *Voices in my head*

Kate McIlhagga

'Well my dear,' the voice said, 'I think you really want to be a minister.' I looked up at the kindly face in the Edinburgh tearoom. 'Do angels wear felt hats?' I wondered. This 'messenger' had been interviewing me on behalf of the Church of Scotland's Deaconess Committee. Through the Iona Community I had become involved in youth work and interested in parish work. I was 22 and in my final year at St Andrew's University. The year was 1960.

A man's voice spoke this time. 'Well, Miss X, are you engaged or planning to get married?' 'None of your business,' interrupted a member of the Iona Community and another member of the panel. I was being interviewed for training as a youth worker with the Church of Scotland.

And so my first taste of ministry began, at Moray House, Edinburgh, with a post-Albemarle course in group dynamics related to youth work and community development. Perhaps being a Glaswegian saw me through the horrors and humiliations of being one of three women in a group of seasoned youth workers exposed to a new concept of training. During that year I learned a great deal about myself, about others and about the principles of community development – knowledge that was to stand me in good stead throughout my ministry. Learning how to be an enabler and facilitator, rather than a person always up front and in charge, laid a strong foundation for future work. Helping people to help themselves rather than diving in and doing it for them was a valuable lesson in process.

After a further year in Edinburgh and Aberdeen working on youth advisory teams it was only 1963 and the Church of Scotland was still not ordaining women.

Tapestry threads

As I look back over 34 years of ministry I can see threads that have remained predominant in the tapestry of my life journey. There is the Iona Community, the ecumenical group which never fails to welcome and affirm, stretch and challenge, with a healthy dose of healing laughter for good measure. There are women's issues: issues of justice and language, sexuality and solidarity. Born out of this is commitment to process and an involvement with and a struggle for a spirituality in a place where prayer and politics meet. There is the strong thread of the influence of the Student Christian Movement, with its commitment to a radical theology, an openness to questioning and doubt and a willingness to be in real dialogue with others. There is the bright thread of family life with all its agony and joy.

Back in 1963 I had other things on my mind. Some friends decided to get their B.D. and hope the church would ordain them eventually. Perhaps I am not made of the stuff of pioneers. I couldn't become a member of the Iona Community because George MacLeod said the loos weren't convenient! So I listened to the heartbeat of God and the dictates of my own instincts and entered the ministry of marriage, to have and to hold, in sickness and in health, for richer for poorer. That has been a real voyage of discovery.

As I reflect on that period in the early '60s, on ground broken, on preparation made for so many things, I realise how much I owe the S.C.M. in enabling me as a woman to take my place in meetings and conferences; to have a say, when so many women's voices went unheard and women themselves were invisible. It was only later that I learned the value of listening as well as having the courage to speak. It was also a period of pressure: the pressure felt by being the first woman to preach in a particular church or to chair a conference. Like most women I had to learn to resist the temptation of trying to be better then my male colleagues in order to prove my worth.

Marriage, ten years, three sons and three part-time LEA youth work jobs later and I was able to reflect on women's ability to juggle: work and worship, nappies and agendas, meetings and mothering, marriage and ministry.

Pentecost tragedy

There was a deep pit at my feet and little room to stand. Anxiously I looked behind me. A low rail saved the day. Hooking my heels over it I committed into God's encompassing presence two vibrant young people tragically killed in a road accident. How that young man would have laughed at the sight of me tottering at the edge of his grave. He was always teasing 'Mrs Vicar'. How she would have smiled at my sensible shoes. She always looked wonderful.

A week before, we had received a phone call in the early hours of Pentecost Sunday. The voice said that there had been a terrible accident and they thought we might know one of those involved. My mind raced round the whereabouts of my nearest and dearest, as the voice continued to name the daughter of a church family and ask if we would accompany the police to inform the family. I felt guilty and relieved, shocked, numb, angry and apprehensive. 'Of course,' I said and arrived (with clothes on back to front I discovered later) at the local police station. 'You may know the others involved in the accident,' they said. We did. A brother and sister in their early twenties, close friends of our family; two more church members. A voice said, 'You can't cry now.' I didn't and for for all the years afterwards when I couldn't, regretted it.

As we drove to the house all I could hear in my head were the words I think Duncan said in *Macbeth*: 'What all, all my dear ones?' It was too much. I stood on the doorstep knowing that once that bell was rung and the door opened to reveal their ministers and a police man and woman standing there at 2 am, life would never be the same for my friends. I wished I could turn back the clock.

That Pentecost began a period in my ministry dominated by death. I reached depths I had never known existed. I shared grief and rage, despair and hope with so many people. I learned that ministers too have to grieve; have to come to terms with loss. Tragedy succeeded tragedy in our town. Too many accidental deaths of children and adults. Each time I preside at a communion service they are there around that table singing, laughing, their faces glowing in the light of candles. Around that time a friend, who had recently attempted suicide, initiated a 'snowdrop' ministry. She showed me how these wonderful white candles of hope contain within them tiny green hearts, a symbol of God's renewing love. The mother of two of the young people killed at Pentecost allowed me to pick an armful from her garden to use at the funeral of a young child.

During this period I was appointed part-time chaplain to our theological college in Cambridge and will always be grateful that staff and students allowed me to bring this appalling agenda to them. Ministry needs support and those training for ministry need to know that. I learned that when I needed help and support most, it was those who had suffered most who had the resources to give it. For example the friend whose brother had recently died who prayed for me as I conducted worship, having just been told of my father's death. The family whose child was undergoing treatment for cancer, who prayed for me as I conducted worship on that Pentecost Sunday. The friend whose husband had left her and whose daughter had attempted suicide, who was there for me when I most needed support.

We preach unconditional love in the church. I've learned the hard way that we don't always receive it, we can't always give it, but those who have suffered most are likely to be those who have the courage and the compassion to be alongside the marginalised and the despairing. When we are hurting and broken we often feel isolated and forsaken. When we are set apart by pain or stigma it takes a special kind of person to pilgrim with us. But when that does happen, we experience the giving and receiving of the vulnerable love that following Christ's way is all about.

Bereavement care

A new year and a new tragedy. A flooded dyke took the lives of a young couple as they tried to rescue their child, who was subsequently swept to the bank where his sister looked on in horror. We had to trace their grandparents' address through our baptism register. Luckily their godparents were local. Family, school and church worked together to help in the next few days – not least to protect them from an intrusive press. I worked with their doctor to issue a press release and found that drawing pictures (of where the two coffins would be in the church) helped grief to flow and encouraged me, if I had not already had enough incentive, to set up a Cruse Bereavement Care branch in our area. With a lot of planning and help a county branch was established two years later and when I left the area it had over twenty-five trained bereavement 'carers', offering support and a listening ear to those who asked for help. Not quite reaping joy from what is sown in pain, but certainly a feeling that out of death can come resurrection and new life. I learned how important it is to grieve, to ask for and accept help, to allow the tapestry of bereavement to be woven: sadness and fear, anger and pain, numbness and searching form its pattern in each individual life until the tasks of mourning are complete. I learned how men, in trying to protect women from pain and unpleasantness, will often deprive them of important grieving tools, like viewing a body where it is appropriate. I learned to be silent in the face of appalling grief and rage, but to be there, to hold and to stay. So many bereaved parents experience the rejection of those who 'don't know what to say' or the insensitivity of those who say, 'I know how you feel.' You don't need words and you can never know how another person feels.

Do women have a special ministry in bereavement? Some do. Some men who are prepared to wait and listen and weep do as well. I also learned during that period that I am not the only minister. I knew it theologically but not in my gut until someone dying mistook a nurse for myself and asked her to pray for her, which she did; until a friend kneeling at the side of her husband, laid out on the floor, led us in prayer so naturally.

So death has shaped my ministry – not least the prospect of my own. I was to be ordained on St Andrew's Day. 'But I'm being ordained,' I said feebly to the group of serious men. 'I can't have cancer. I haven't got time for operations.' 'The lump is malignant,' was the reply. I went white, the student red, my husband green and the surgeon's black face remained sympathetic but firm. They were very good at reassuring me about the wonders of breast prosthesis, but not too hot on talking about what I wanted to talk about – the dreaded C word. How often those in the caring profession answer the unasked questions while ignoring the deeper pleas for help.

Three months and several sessions of radiotherapy later I was ordained and inducted to a part-time post of Community Minister in a thriving market town in East Anglia, twenty-one years after the first voice had planted the seed of a call deep within me. After thirteen years of marriage, motherhood and part-time youth and community work I had finally candidated for the ministry and became a full member of the Iona Community.

Yorkshire youth

Our first home had been in Leeds where my husband worked on the staff of the Student Christian Movement. I found work on the youth club staff of a large comprehensive school. We moved to Sheffield fifteen months later. So often in Christian marriage the call of one leaves the other to follow (or not) and find work if they are fortunate enough in a new area. Nowadays not even ministers move about the country without taking into account the needs and aspirations of their spouses. It would be thirty years before I was the one to receive the call and my husband had to find new avenues of ministry in a new community.

But back to Sheffield. I had had a miscarriage the previous year so was overjoyed when after a long labour our first son was born. Number two son arrived when we had moved from the curate's flat near the Jessop Hospital for Women to the Michael

Church on a large housing estate. In a new church with a lively group of first generation Christians there were no expectations of the 'minister's wife' so I was able to offer in ministry the gifts and training I had, rather than meet stereotyped needs. I will always be grateful for the support of other women in that congregation, who became sisters and surrogate grannies. When lack of sleep drove me mad there was always someone there. I hope we supported each other in that period, although my memories are much more of receiving than of giving. That in itself was a valuable lesson. When the boys were in school and nursery I looked for part-time employment, not least because one wage didn't keep a family in shoes and we were dependent on the generosity of parents for holidays and treats of any kind. There was still work to be found at that period but the erosion of confidence that motherhood entails for some had undermined any ability to see myself in a positive light. I hope I was a good enough mother, but motherhood seemed to have swamped selfhood. I was to remember that when, in later years as a counsellor, I listened to the stories of other women.

Two years' part-time youth work with Youth Action helped to redress the balance and laid down yet another layer of training and experience for ministry. I was working with schools and liaising with social work agencies, placing and supporting young people in voluntary projects. This had developed from involvement in a summer play scheme project in the local park, where older youngsters worked in a team to enable younger children to explore all manner of things through art and games, sport and craft. I learned the amount of sound administration that needs to go into an enabling project. Listening and responding to peoples' needs and facilitating leadership in others requires the underpinning of an attention to detail which I didn't always have. (The learning curve continues as, over twenty years later, I still struggle with the finances, building needs and interminable rotas of three small village churches.) Having your own children involved in your work tests the patience of any worker. How to balance fairness with affirmation is not always easy and not much different from the need to prioritise experienced by everyone in pastoral ministry.

Ecumenical parish

Seven years' hard work behind us and a move was suggested to a new village being built outside Cambridge. It seemed a risk and it certainly was a culture shock, but all that was outweighed by the exciting ecumenical possibilities. Five denominations were working and worshipping together. They met initially in a site hut, then in the school, moving eventually to their own purpose-built centre. Once more the constraints of one person's call defined the opportunities for the other. I was fortunate to find work on the staff of the local village college and to be asked to set up a village club in our own village.

New jobs and a new house that had a garden led inevitably to a new baby to make our family complete. Again the support of other families, the baby-sitting circle, the suitcase of baby and children's clothes that circulated created a supportive community in the absence of an extended family. As a grandmother now of three years' standing I regret that my children saw so little of their grandparents. So for us, as for so many other families and singles, the church becomes 'home community'. What a responsibility to be open to friend and stranger, to offer and accept hospitality, to be inclusive rather than exclusive.

The expectations of Congregationalists and Methodists, of Quakers and Baptists, of Presbyterians and Anglicans were as varied as were their views of what role their minister's spouse should fulfil. My reflection on that period is that the greatest divide was theological rather than denominational. The mud and muddle of a new community brought us together in adversity. We struggled to speak the truth in love, to understand each other, to entertain forgiveness and the possibility of change. Of such stuff are ecumenical parishes made. The initial developers of the village had built in community enclaves with plenty of play space and walkways. When they sold out, the second phase of building reverted to straight roads and crescents, and houses with chimneys, albeit no open fires! Perhaps it was the mud, the lack of resources, the open plan living that brought the pioneers closer together.

Perhaps it was the inevitable outcome of growth that, although buildings had been happily shared in the beginning, as the village grew each group needed its own place and space. So where before school and church centre had housed youth and children's work, health and sports facilities, the map when we left boasted Scout Hut, Play Group Hut, Health Centre and Youth Centre. Even so, during these years I learned the valuable lesson of how partnership between, for example, the health service and the church is not only helpful but essential. For this to happen in a creative way the church and its staff have to have credibility amongst their peers.

During those four demanding years, before and after the birth of our third son, I took my courage in both hands and asked for help to work on myself; to understand my periodic bouts of depression, which I could no longer kid myself were merely post-natal. This experience has led to a whole new field of opportunity and ministry. Out of something that felt very negative and unfruitful came the possibility of growth and positive tools for the future – I later trained as a counsellor myself.

Money for the 'Free Church' appointment in the Local Ecumenical Project ran out after four years and we had to look for somewhere else to live and work. The United Reformed Church had just come into being, uniting Presbyterians and Congregationalists. We were offered work in suburban areas, which didn't seem the radical option for those involved in the Iona Community and committed to working on the margins. It took a long time to shed the inverted snobbery of someone who always failed to mention that her family home between the years of thirteen and university had been in Bearsden, an affluent suburb of Glasgow! A short period working on Iona filled in a gap before we finally moved north.

Market town student

It wasn't the 'proper' north, just seven miles up the road to a market town which had grown from 3,000 to 15,000 in a remarkably short

time. The church, a Victorian Gothic building, dominated the centre
of the market place. Money for the spire had been given by a
wealthy mill owner on the understanding that it should be several
feet taller than the 12th-century parish church situated at the old
village centre by a ford across the river Ouse. It was. To come to a
dark building, whose heavy wooden doors were only open for an
hour on a Sunday, after the space and light of a modern church
centre was not easy. The church however is not the building but
the people and, as with people anywhere, there were needs and
hopes, opportunities and apathy, deeply ingrained prejudice and
forward-looking vision expressed by those who called my
husband. I rapidly learned that, as well as receiving many kind-
nesses, things were expected of me. How I dressed, the role I
played in women's work seemed to have been written into a
hidden script, which I was expected to know. I learned the
enabling power of the two-letter word 'no'. If the expected person
says 'no' to a task, there may be a time of disappointment but
inevitably and usually there emerges someone far better able than
the 'minister's wife' to play that role. The early years of a twenty-
year period were not easy. Come to think of it, nor were the middle
or the last years. I eventually found work out in the Fens running
a village youth club three nights a week. For the seventy young
people arriving on their bikes it was a good place to meet and
socialise until the pub became a more natural venue. As the music
decibels rose and opportunities to interact diminished I realised my
youth work days had come to an end.

Time off at new year led to a rare interlude of marital discussion. Where did our future lie? 'I think you should apply to train for
the ministry at Westminster College in Cambridge' – the voice of my
husband this time. 'Do angels wear woolly jumpers?' I wondered. I
took some persuading. Was it a case of 'if you can't beat 'em join
'em'? How could I go back to academic work after fifteen years? I
don't think it crossed my mind that I might be turned down! Not I
hope because I was arrogant enough to think I was God's gift to
ministry, but because the certainty of the wisdom of the Voice had
settled deep into the core of my being. So on the day that our

youngest son started school I entered the process of having my call tested by the church at different levels.

'Who will cook your husband's breakfast if you go to college?' someone asked at the Church Meeting, which had to commend me. That hurdle over, I was duly commended and despatched to an interview in London. 'Be yourself,' advised a friend as we met in the corridors of power. Somehow I must have satisfied them that I could cope with a family and commuting to Cambridge to study theology for three years. Writing five-thousand-word essays while cooking for five certainly concentrated the mind. Approval of having a student as a mum or a mum as a student was mixed – from 'Go for it' to 'Don't you think one in the family is quite enough?'! The son who told his friends that I worked down the pub shall remain nameless.

I discovered many things as a student. I'd been a Universalist all my life and hadn't known it. The S.C.M. had provided a solid grounding not only in theology, but also in the ability to question and discuss. The Iona Community had trained me well in incarnational theology and in spirituality that saw no division between work and worship, prayer and politics.

Not so much a community centre . . .

During my three years of commuting to Cambridge my home church was going through an enormous sea change. Plans had been passed, after a great deal of research and preparation, to gut the building, to put a floor in with access by lift and to incorporate commercial premises on the ground floor which would bring in rent until the church could afford to take them back. It was the conversion of a building and a people from Victorian triumphalism to a servant theology which would meet the needs of the 1980s. The forbidding wooden doors approached by a flight of steps were replaced by glass ones at street level. There was now smooth access for anyone into the warm and welcoming foyer. A small chapel for prayer was retained in the outer foyer. This came to be used for daily worship by centre staff, members of other churches and anyone out shopping or passing by. Over the years a ministry of intercessory prayer for the sick evolved and we had many requests to pray for all sorts of situations. We encouraged those who asked for prayer to come and pray with us. We were not trying to change God's mind, but placing ourselves alongside those who were sick or suffering, knowing that the healing Christ was there already. Those who were housebound or unable to join us knew that at 10 am each morning someone would be keeping watch with them. A rota of people was responsible for this important ministry at a time suitable for old and young, staff and passers-by. It was much more difficult to initiate an evening office.

A functional hall and kitchen led off the foyer and the ground floor plan was completed by a lounge, which older members remembered had been used for the reception of evacuees during the last war, and a room for a medibath and hairdressing. These facilities were used by the four-day-a-week Day Care Centre, which had an important place in the refurbished building. The elderly and housebound came by car or ambulance to a centre which offered social support, some medical services like chiropody and the hospitality of a loving group of volunteers from all parts of the local community. They met upstairs in the 'Centrum' which was also where concerts and exhibitions were held and worship celebrated week by week. The lift took pushchairs and coffins, wheelchairs and people upstairs. After a few years, when debts had been paid off, the ground floor commercial premises were reincorporated into the Church Centre, providing an office for the regional Christian Aid worker, a Traidcraft outlet called 'Just Sharing' and a church office, able and willing to welcome visitors and carry out in an accessible way all the administrative tasks of such a venture.

My husband was asked to give 50% of his time to this exciting model of mission. It was important that the centre did not become isolated from the ongoing life of the worshipping community. This released a part-time ministry post. It was decided to appoint a Community Minister, who would liaise with the groups who became part of the church centre community, while keeping their concerns firmly on the agenda of the worshipping community. Although the model was clearly more 'community service' than 'community development' the skills and philosophy of the latter were being applied. Community Minister in my own church – was this what all these years of preparation were leading to?

It was the end of term, and most of my fellow students had received a call to a church. The choices were stark. Either we both moved elsewhere, or I remained and worked in an unofficial way, or I applied for the job, which could have been made for someone with my community education background. I agonised for weeks until a voice said, 'It may feel like a plot, but if it's a plot of the Holy Spirit ...' I applied. I was interviewed by a Church Meeting of forty-six and while they conferred I climbed the ladder to the almost completed Centrum and knew it was right. Fortunately the Church Meeting agreed. I was finally ordained at the end of January 1981, twenty-one years after that first 'Voice' had 'jaloused a call'. Had I or the church or both at last come of age? Looking back, it is always possible to suspect God's hand in the decisions and directions of life, to sense God's use of the mistakes and God's presence in the despair.

... More a centre of community

For thirteen years my ministry was focused on the community. My visiting was dictated as much by the request of a health visitor or doctors as by elders' lists. It was a ministry as part of a team of ministerial colleagues and later students in training from whom I learned a great deal. Team ministry is very demanding if it is to work properly. It demands consultation without multiplying meetings, clarity of role without being too rigid about demarcation lines, and an ability for married couples to separate personal agenda from public. By all means disagree with your spouse at a meeting but not because he or she forgot to put the rubbish out again. Be as polite or rude to your spouse as you would be to any other member of the team. We all bring baggage to a meeting.

Couples have to be aware of this. For me, however, the key to good team work has always been honesty and forgiveness. If there appears to be tension, sit down and talk about it. Go and see the person concerned. Admit your fault. Try to stand in the other person's shoes and for God's sake offer and accept forgiveness. A sense of humour helps! For far too long ministers have been put on pedestals and then if they fall or fail they are crucified. Ministers have a specific role to play but so do teachers, counsellors, caretakers, secretaries and prophets, to name but a few. If any of the above become too full of their own importance the whole team is thrown out of balance.

My work was alongside all sorts of different teams and groups. Hopefully it was an enabling ministry, encouraging and resourcing others; believing that they could do something and affirming them in what they did. I too needed that affirmation and was pleased that the role required a support group. In my experience it is important to distinguish between support of the person and support of the work. When a church opens wide its doors physically and its arms theologically it issues an invitation, which if responded to means sacrificial caring, endless listening and good management of time. The use of the two-letter word became essential. All of us who work in the caring professions need to know that we need to be needed. Everybody does. The balance however is important. If our need overtakes our response to others something is seriously wrong. Good supervision and spiritual direction can act as a counterbalance in this delicate balancing act. Few ministers of my acquaintance avail themselves of what is a requirement in other professions.

Helping to build up the life of the Church Centre community was exciting and exhausting. Reminding others of the need for ownership by all groups and not just the church was not always understood. Balancing that with regular preaching was a challenge. I was the first woman to preach in that church and there were undoubtedly prejudices to overcome in the early days. Stress in ministry is at last being acknowledged and dealt with. For some it has been almost a badge of office. Admitting vulnerability is impossible for others. How hard and how painful it is to reach the sort of relationship with others where you can be completely yourself. In the 80s it was still the perceived wisdom that ministers should not make friends within the congregation. That can create an incredibly lonely scenario. I have always accepted friendship when offered, tried to return it, have often failed and frequently been disillusioned. In the end of the day the friends who are there for each other despite everything have proved the difference between friend and acquaintance. We are called to love one another. That doesn't mean living in each other's pockets or even liking each other. It has much more to do with the costly love which stretched out arms on a cross. Or as a telly programme put it, 'Love Hurts'. We would be naive to think otherwise.

Chaplaincies three

In the early years of my appointment as Community Minister I occasionally became involved with worship at the nearby Peace Camp. We often had campers and RAF and USAF personnel in the congregation. My sermons were always biblical.

As the years went by the job grew. A part-time chaplaincy at my old theological college was added. With five ministers on staff, was a chaplain really necessary? The students thought so. Occupying the middle ground was not easy, but an enabling ministry was clearly needed. At that time the average age of students was 43, so the community was made up of women and men of mature years, who had left security and sometimes family behind to train for ministry. They brought experience and skills but often felt de-skilled. They sometimes brought watertight theological systems and often felt betrayed. As we moved into the Decade of Churches in Solidarity with Women (1988–98) the Cambridge Federation of Theological Colleges was rightly addressing the issues of sexism and inclusive language. Many new students had not encountered the thought of either before. My ministry there was, I think, increasingly valued as I moved over the years from working in the Common Room, where I hung around drinking coffee for the sake of the kingdom, to having a room of my own, where people felt they could talk in confidence. I valued the students' ministry to me and the increasing sense of working in a team with my colleagues on staff. The language and culture of a theological college were not alien to me. Later short-term appointments to chaplaincy work at an RAF station and a hospital took me into foreign countries.

An RAF station that flew desks not planes was indeed unexplored territory for a member of Christian CND. For a woman, a pacifist, even to contemplate that role was interesting to say the least, but my tutor on my counselling course, himself a full-time assistant chaplain-in-chief, encouraged me. I urged him to change the visiting cards issued to all chaplains so that they were printed in inclusive language. He did. The place was confusing, the jargon was confusing; the language, the ethos, the culture all left me wanting to turn and run. So must the outsider to a church community feel! There was, however, work to be done. I was shown enormous courtesy and kindness overcoming many barriers when, as many times before, I confessed my ignorance about procedures and customs. Of course the paternalism is hard to deal with. The rate of marriage breakdown was high, as were the expectations of women to conform to certain roles. Here was familiar ground. After four years there I finished on a high, being asked to propose the toast to the immortal memory of Robert Burns at the Squadron's Burns' Supper. It's amazing how much about peace-making there is in Burns if you look hard enough. A terrifying experience but a woman's a woman for a' that.

The hospital chaplaincy was different again. The chaplain entered several communities under one roof. Keeping track of patients was almost impossible. Blink and they had been discharged. The staff remained, doing long shifts and facing increasing amounts of paperwork. The RAF had taught me that I was being retained till needed. It was actually all right to hang around, to loiter with intent. I would be called on if and when the time was right, but only if I had earned the trust of the other staff.

On one or two occasions I had the privilege of becoming involved in the life of patients or staff. I learned a great deal from the experience. Giving people permission to talk at a deeper level when they were ready was important. Making the time to listen, hearing what was said, not making assumptions, being used as a reconciler and asking before praying were all part of the learning curve. I made a lot of mistakes and many friends. Hospitals now see ecumenical teams working alongside medical teams. The chaplain is a highly professional member of staff with skills to offer alongside those of social workers, nurses, doctors and even consultants. Regarded in the past as 'gods in white coats', doctors' training has allowed them to become much more people-friendly while still maintaining a professional objectivity when needed. Ministers also need to know about boundaries. For us this is much more difficult and we often cross them, slip over them or are tempted to transgress them. Ministers, it may surprise you to hear, are human.

It was not the hospital or the RAF or the Church Centre which provided the most recent voice in my head but the college. I had been involved in the preparation for an international conference in Sheffield on the 'Community of Women and Men in the Church'. That WCC programme had evolved from a study of sexism in the 70s and had been the most widely taken up of all such projects, not least because women worldwide are caught up in a web of oppression, from violence and poverty to sexism and unemployment. I was asked to preach at the college commemoration service. A doubtful privilege, I thought, as I wore a hole in the principal's carpet prior to the service. I took the text of the woman at the well and attempted to 'sock it to 'em' on a hot June day when I was the only person in reach of a glass of water! Afterwards a senior woman minister spoke to me. My generation has few women role models so it was good to talk with someone older. 'Come and see me when you next travel north,' she said. I thought she lived in Seascale on the northwest coast. It turned out she lived in Seahouses on the northeast. I had told her that the juggling act of three (part-time – in theory) jobs was becoming too much. I duly visited and learned that she was about to retire and that ministers were needed in north Northumberland, to work in groups, to set up a fascinating 'mission to tourists project' on Holy Island and to develop retreat work. All of these appealed enormously, but were we ready to move after nearly twenty-five years in East Anglia? Our children were fortunate to have found jobs and homes elsewhere. I found the pull back to the north very strong. When there are two people looking for work, trying to follow a 'call' or to seek God's will, it isn't always straightforward. The Holy Spirit has a way of brooding over our chaos, however, and bringing light out of darkness.

The 'Secret Kingdom'

After a period of dislocation, pain and intense bereavement, I found myself being interviewed on a cold winter's evening in the wilds of Northumberland. As the elders conferred and I stood outside what was to become our home I knew it was right. Fortunately the elders did as well. I was invited to 'preach with a view', which I did in the January, thirteen years almost to the day since my ordination. I also attended a Burns Supper to hear the bitter-sweet love songs of the Bard played on the Northumberland pipes for the first time. When the phone call came calling me to the north the family produced champagne and toasted Mum's new job. They seemed to be quite proud of the old girl. I reflected on the fact that I had exchanged three part-time jobs for three rural churches. Who says God hasn't got a sense of humour!

I moved to St Cuthbert's Manse on St Cuthbert's Day. It was good to see three good men and true busy hoovering the place as the furniture van rolled up. The first few months were difficult. Living in such a beautiful part of the country within sight of hills and sea hardly compensated for the loss of family, friends and familiar support networks. Nearly four years on, with new friendships and networks forged, the stresses are different. Most of the churches in Northumberland, of any denomination, are struggling to remain viable. The URC is no exception. Ecumenical relationships are good, and inclusive language is becoming known. Over the years infrastructures have become weak. The struggle to remain solvent often supersedes any energy for community work or mission.

I have recently been appointed a 'District Minister' until I retire in six years' time. One church is putting its buildings (including our manse) up for sale and we move in the summer to a refurbished manse owned by the District in another village. The congregation here will continue, worshipping in the parish church across the road. Another congregation faces difficult decisions about buildings and survival. The third is working hard to build up contact with families and to work alongside Anglicans and Methodists in the village. The skills needed here seem to be those of structural engineer, electrician, plumber, accountant and builder – or at least knowing where to find such help. One church secretary is seconded from a nearby town church. People here have different expectations of ministry and are gradually learning that we too have times of relaxation or despair; that we need time with our family and that we can only be available if we are invited into homes and lives. On reflection, perhaps the skills of a bereavement counsellor and one-time chaplain are just what are needed in these difficult times for small congregations.

The 'Holy Island Project', with which I am involved as convenor of its management committee, has a director in post and plans to refurbish the 19th-century church as a retreat and pilgrim centre offering hospitality as Cuthbert did to those thirsty in a dry land, who come on pilgrimage to 'this place'. A sabbatical in 1992 had taken me on an eight-day silent retreat to St Bueno's in Wales and since then I have come more and more to value silence and retreat as a way into active prayer. Through the Iona Community's 'Rediscovery of Spirituality' area of concern group, I have come to see that the way we do things is as important as what we do; that prayer is like sex: we kid ourselves that others are having more of it and doing it better than we are.

Here in Northumbria's 'Secret Kingdom' the rhythm of creation lends itself to a deep celebration of the ebb and flow of the Christian year. How meaningful the lights of Advent will be at the end of a dark and wild November. Nature's white candles of hope, the snowdrops, will appear for Candlemas, growing even on the dunes.

So, nearly 40 years on, the Iona Community still plays a key role in my life and ministry. It's good to live in the borderlands and to be receiving the unconditional love and support we pledge to give each other. I've found the same willingness to walk alongside at the nearby Franciscan house and have learned much from the acceptance of the Brothers, whose work in this area is much appreciated.

From an Edinburgh teashop to a Franciscan refectory is a far cry. From learning to write on a slate to producing this on computer is a major leap. From a city park to a Fenland village, a housing estate to a new community, a market town to a rural fishing village is quite a pilgrimage. All has been ministry: all has been part of the ministry of the whole people of God. God is present in every blessed thing and place; present in friend and stranger; present in the voids, the absences and the silent terrors of the night. Going on pilgrimage certainly changes the pilgrim. Setting out in faith is never easy, but for richer and for poorer, in sickness and in health still holds for ministry as it does for marriage.

6 *Whose I am and whom I serve*

Katharine Poulton

'Why don't you think of reading theology?' The question posed to me by an old family friend in the autumn of 1979 was to have far reaching consequences as I considered my choice of university course and my future life. When I went to Manchester University in 1980 to read theology, I was the first person from my school to have studied the subject at degree level. Little did I know that this 'first' was to be the beginning of many.

Going to university in England or Scotland or Wales is not unusual for young people from Northern Ireland. The 'brain drain' has become quite a problem as many fail to return. Although many of my friends 'crossed the water' I know of only one other who, like me, returned home. My return was to herald the beginning of a process that would take me on a path I had never anticipated. Like many, I had always expected that I would teach – it seemed to be a respectable career, the holidays were good, and any teachers I had known were happy. But this was not to be.

As a student in Manchester, I enjoyed life very much, although I did find it different to the life I had led at home. Involved in church activities all my life and growing up in a semi-rural Ulster community, I found it hard to get used to the idea that the people I now lived with and who were my friends did not go near church. I tried the university chaplaincy, but found it difficult to integrate there. The 'student' churches in the area were also far removed from my limited experience of church life. If I went to church at all during my first year as an undergraduate it was to the folk mass in the local Roman Catholic church: a new experience for one born and bred in Ulster, and not something to be broadcast at home. During my second year, I lived with some friends in the Hulme area of Manchester. It was a tough area and crime was widespread. But it was here, in the Anglican Church of the Ascension where I became a regular worshipping member of the congregation, that the call to the ordained ministry came. It was, however, by no means clear how I might fulfil that call. In 1982 the Anglican churches in the United Kingdom looked far from ordaining women. Perhaps I would be a teacher after all! In 1983 I graduated, married Ian and returned to Northern Ireland, where I worked for the Northern Ireland Housing Executive. This was a job which I enjoyed, I made some friends to whom I would minister later on and, more importantly at the time, it brought in money for us, since Ian had gone to Dublin to train for the ordained ministry of the Church of Ireland. I knew from contacts with various people that the Church of Ireland might well consider ordaining women as deacons, but it was all very low key and there was no movement for the ordination of women pressing for this step to be taken.

In May 1984, the General Synod of the Church of Ireland took the momentous step of passing all necessary legislation to allow women to be ordained to the diaconate in the Church of Ireland. Later that year I spent three days at a selection conference and was permitted to begin training for the ordained ministry in September 1985. I was the first woman to go forward and the first to begin training. It was all quite a surprise to me, not that I was actually going to be allowed to do something which I had been called by God to do, but because so much attention was being focused on me. I had gone through the whole process of being accepted for training with many worries. Knowing that Ian was already in Dublin and would be ordained a year ahead of me was one of my concerns, but the first of our practical problems was to materialise much sooner than this. Where would we, as a married couple, live? The very male theological college could not and would not (at that time) accommodate a married couple. We were advised to look for a flat at a 'non-commercial rate'. This was a virtual impossibility in Dublin, a young growing city where premium rates for flats are the norm. However, we were fortunate in finding two rooms over a garage in a private home, within cycling distance of the college, and we lived there for a year.

When Ian was ordained for the curacy of Newtownards in Co. Down it meant that once again we were separated. I was unhappy at the prospect of having to live outside the college and worked hard negotiating with the principal and other members of staff to be given a room inside. Another woman, Kathleen Young, had come to train and we had adjoining rooms with sinks! After all, these men were to be our colleagues in ministry. Had we been made to live elsewhere we would not really have known our fellow students. Many people thought that there would have been vociferous opposition to women training for the ordained ministry and that Kathleen and I would have found great solace in pouring out our troubles to each other. Disappointingly for some, it was not like this for us. We integrated into the life of the college and rarely went into each other's rooms. We had our own friends and our academic and practical work to keep us busy. In all aspects of college life we were fairly treated and allowed to play as full a part as anyone else. More than ten years on, male colleagues can reminisce about life in college with me: something which I feel is very important and gives a sense of belonging and bonding. Being an ordained minister can in so many aspects be an isolating experience.

In June 1987 I was ordained deacon to serve in the parish of Bangor, Co. Down, only a short hop down the road from our home in Newtownards. At least this seemed a good start.

Being the first woman ordained in the Church of Ireland brought many difficulties. I had not anticipated such media interest in my ordination, in my 'story', in my problems. I found it very hard to cope with the constant stream of requests from newspapers, television and radio and I would say that this of all was my greatest challenge in being ordained for ministry in the Church of Ireland. The media interest was aroused because in England there was so much publicity given to the women who were being ordained, and there was deep division within the church. My ordination was to be a momentous day, not only for me, but for the Church of Ireland, and I did not want it to be destroyed by anyone – particularly not by any journalist who might try to make the event seem something that would split the church. In the event, the media did turn out, but I was relieved that the ordination merely warranted a short slot on a tea time news programme.

The Church of Ireland is a relatively small member of the Anglican Communion with about 360,000 members. It is a widely scattered and generally conservative church. Disestablished from the Church of England in 1870, the Church of Ireland is proud of its structures and ability to carry out its own administrative and synodical business. The Church of Ireland is the Anglican church for the whole island of Ireland. Some dioceses and indeed some parishes straddle the political border so that in some churches the prayers may be for the Queen and the royal family, while in the other church of the parish the prayers may be for the President. The majority of Church of Ireland people live in Northern Ireland, with the largest concentrations in the counties of Armagh, Down and Antrim. In the West of Ireland, in counties such as Mayo, Galway and Clare, Church of Ireland numbers are tiny and it is a struggle for many churches to keep their doors open. Until 1987, when I was ordained as deacon, the Church of Ireland had no tradition of women ministering. Occasionally in a large urban parish there may have been a Church Army sister or a 'commissioned lady worker', or perhaps a lay reader would have helped take occasional parts of services, but there was no history of women serving in permanent positions. So it was all very new for everybody. Those who were opposed to the ordination of women – and there were some, both clerical and lay – were quiet. It is my feeling that, because there had been no women's pressure groups, no vociferous protests at General Synod meetings, those who opposed decided to do the decent thing and wait to see how women fitted into the very male-dominated world of the Church of Ireland ministry. Perhaps, too, the fact that women were to remain as deacons for the foreseeable future helped to ease the consciences of those who did not think women should be ordained to the priesthood. This meant that the men who were ordained with me would be ordained priest after a year as deacons, and so could do those things denied to a deacon (and therefore to a woman) – celebrate the Eucharist, give a blessing, carry out a wedding. It also meant that women would not be able to progress up the 'career ladder', if we can use such terms of the Christian ministry, since most parishes would be seeking a priest who could carry out all the necessary functions without having to bring in help from outside.

Being ordained as a deacon gave me plenty of scope. Apart from those functions mentioned above, all other aspects of ministry were possible: pastoral care in many forms, evangelism, service in schools, in the community, anywhere in fact that there were people. And despite the fact that there were clergy who wavered and quietly felt uneasy or even opposed to women being ordained, it is true to say that no one ever took their feelings out personally on me and relationships with other clergy were always and remain good.

Bangor parish, where my ministry began was (and is) a large parish by Church of Ireland standards, with around a thousand families. There was also a 'daughter church' in a new housing area, a local ecumenical project with the Methodists. My arrival in Bangor naturally provoked some curiosity and whilst some members of the congregation had quietly voiced their misgivings to the rector, no one waved any placards in objection. 'Quite disappointing,' remarked the rector's wife.

I was allowed to integrate into the life and witness of the parish in a normal way and found that by simply working hard people saw that I was someone who had a calling, a vocation to serve and who tried to carry it out as well as I could. I always felt that by working hard and by letting as wide a variety of people as possible experience the ministry of women for themselves, we would gradually become a very normal and natural part of the ordained ministry of our church. As the first slow trickle of women came into the diaconate of the Church of Ireland, that is what happened, and as we worked away, behind the scenes, others – the legislators and the movers – smoothed the path for the General Synod to debate the issue of women priests. In 1990 the necessary legislation for women to be ordained to the priesthood was passed. In that year, Kathleen Young and the late Irene Templeton were ordained priests: not only the first in Ireland, but in the British Isles. My ordination to the priesthood was delayed until the spring of 1991, following the birth of Michael.

Women's ministry in the Church of Ireland was by now widely accepted and seen as a valued and valuable aspect of our Christian life and witness. The Church of Ireland may be slow at accepting change, people may still cling to that which is familiar, such as the *Book of Common Prayer*, but there is a parallel reality where change is acknowledged and welcomed and this has been seen in the way women priests have become so widely accepted. Throughout Ireland there are now women priests working in a variety of settings. Some are rectors of parishes, others school chaplains, diocesan youth advisors, curate assistants. On the surface it all looks as though it has been plain sailing, but this has not always been the case.

When the Church of Ireland made the decision to ordain women, way back in 1984, the impression was given that the practicalities would be sorted out as time went by. I have already mentioned some of these, which we faced as theological college students. The deployment of women was, many thought, going to be a problem. Not all rectors would be happy to train women, not all parishes would want to have a woman as rector. In reality, though, the women coming forward for ordination have been women with ability. That was quickly recognised and taken note of, and so many rectors were determined to have women come and serve their first curacies with them. Women have gone as rectors to parishes too, though not all of us seek to take that path at present for a variety of reasons. The main problem of deployment has been with 'clergy couples', of which we were again the first. Although our current situation is most satisfactory, it was not always thus, and the battle is far from over for others.

Following Ian's curacy in Newtownards, he was appointed as rector of three small rural parishes close to Downpatrick. Following Michael's arrival, I was appointed as curate to the rector of Seagoe parish in Portadown, some forty-five miles from home. The rector, David Chillingworth, and myself devised a system of 'sessional working', quite unheard of in our pastorally oriented church, but absolutely necessary in this situation. When I was in the parish I was working, when I was at home I was not on call, unless there was absolutely no one else to deal with the emergency. And when this did occur on a handful of occasions I went off, alone, and once in the middle of the night to minister to a dying man. No one would be able to say that this system of working left any parishioner without pastoral care when they needed it, or that having a woman working in the parish left people without spiritual support in times of need.

Portadown is a town that has become famous for all the wrong reasons, being the focus for the now infamous July Orange Parade to and from Drumcree church. The Parish of Seagoe has always had very strong community, cross-community and ecumenical links. There was plenty of opportunity, both formal and informal to try to nurture good relationships, to build bridges and to discuss the problems which Christian clergy faced in trying to minister in a town which was becoming increasingly divided. Part of the parish incorporated the large, mainly loyalist housing estate of Killicomaine. We had a church hall and youth centre there with plenty of activity most days and nights of the week. The small number of folk who came to the Sunday service there indicated just how far from the church many people were, and it was very hard to try to muster any enthusiasm from the majority of people.

That Sunday congregation consisted of mainly elderly people: people who were very set in their ways and who, I believe, welcomed me as a woman priest because it forged what they perceived to be an even bigger wedge between the Anglican Church in Ireland and the Roman Catholic Church. This was brought home to me when I was asked by the local committee of the Women's World Day of Prayer to lead the annual service, which in that particular year was to be held in the Roman Catholic church in the town centre. I agreed, because I felt there was no better way of developing friendship than taking part in such a service, which would attract a large number of women who might never otherwise have met together. The result of this was that, for the first time in my life, I found myself to be on the receiving end of sectarian hatred. The handful of folk who worshipped in our hall in Killicomaine were very angry at my decision: some decided not to speak to me and followed me up from the hall to where I would lead the worship to vent their anger. The pianist also came in for this verbal abuse when she stated her support for what I was doing. I told the people that they were invited to come along to the service but they were having none of it and one even remarked that she hoped I wouldn't be 'sucked in' – whatever that was supposed to mean. How disappointed I was at their reaction, after all the years of teaching people the Christian way and promoting and providing cross-community contacts. However, I went along and many parishioners who worshipped at the parish church did accompany me. Some were apprehensive about going. They had never been inside a Roman Catholic church before and did not know what to expect. But the service was moving and all felt fulfilled by their experience. That service and a cross-community Passion Play helped pave the way for further cross-community efforts, and during the Week of Prayer for Christian Unity there was an exchange of lay people to read scripture and lead prayers. It might seem trivial to those who live outside the Northern Ireland situation, but in Portadown this was a huge leap forward.

In May 1996, we moved to Larne, Co. Antrim, where Ian became rector. For many people travelling to the Province, Larne is the first place they see, being the terminus for the ferry boats which ply their way from Stranraer and Cairnryan in Scotland. Leaving the gentle, rolling countryside of Co. Down for the rugged coast of Co. Antrim came as quite a shock to all our systems. This move meant uprooting our two children, Michael and Miriam. Following Miriam's arrival in 1993, I had decided to work part-time. This again was a first and there was no provision for it within our church. There had not been any provision for maternity leave either, until I began to investigate and the authorities agreed that parishes had to allow their women clergy the statutory provisions laid down by whichever jurisdiction they resided in. My decision to work part-time came because I found the daily routine of travelling, ministering and being a mother too much to cope with. Six days a week and around six hundred miles' driving was all too much and I felt that something had to go. Having always been conscious of being the 'first' of the women clergy, I did not want anyone to think that I was ducking out of my responsibilities as a priest. But, to be true to the way I felt and to give time to the children I knew something had to change. Ian was very good with helping around the house and with the children, and while we had a good childminder I still wanted to have more time with the children. I was a bit apprehensive about making the switch. I did not want anyone saying that it was evidently a waste of time, money and effort training and ordaining women. But I had also come to the realisation that the other women who had come along behind me were sorting out positions to suit their particular family situations. Ian completely supported what I wanted to do. David Chillingworth was fully behind me, feeling that he would rather have me for half the time than not at all. The Bishop also gave his consent. There were practical considerations too, though, the main one being that, because I would no longer earn the approved minimum stipend, I could no longer be a member of the church pension scheme. This situation would, I was assured, be looked into and resolved as the church authorities investigated new patterns of ministry which were likely to emerge. The issue has not been resolved however, but I prefer not to worry about it, as I am anxious to do what I do and have time with my children. The criticism could be made that there is no such thing as part-time ministry; that clergy must be available all the time. I work with and minister to people as anyone else does, although I may work fewer hours and am paid considerably less. Nor do I enjoy any of the 'perks' such as a free house.

Our move to Larne meant another rethink. Portadown was no further away than it had been from Bright, but the roads were busier. Ian was going to be busier too in his much bigger parish and would not have time to help with child-rearing, school runs and housework. Larne, though predominantly a Presbyterian town, has two Church of Ireland parishes. The rector of the other one, Robert Jones, expressed an interest in having me work with him. His parish needed an extra pair of hands, but could not afford anyone full-time. It seemed like the ideal solution. Telling David was hard, especially as the other member of our team in Seagoe had just been appointed as a rector. In the event, we left within a week of each other, leaving David with a whole winter of work to face by himself. But, now that I live in the community where I minister, I find what I do even more fulfilling and enriching.

The parish bears a lengthy name, but consists of a large housing estate on the edge of Larne, where a forty-year-old church building is the focal point; a small country church serves a rural and semi-rural commuter community; and there is a nissen-hut church hall in a small community. When people realise that a woman is coming to minister in their church, they are very curious. Because of the male domination of our church, this is not surprising, but in Northern Ireland the women are the stalwarts of any congregation, the ones who cater, clean and care, the ones who worship and work for their church and the ones who pray. I arrived in my present parish just as the rector went off ill for a four-month spell. I knew no one, I knew nothing about the pattern of worship. I had not even seen inside the church buildings. But, despite all this, I immediately felt at home with the people. Their ready acceptance of me, their feeling that God had sent me just at the right time to help them through a difficult period, all helped me to settle in very quickly. Who or what folk expected, I do not know, but when I overheard the comment 'She's very ordinary,' I realised that many of them had been quite wound up and expecting this woman priest to be extraordinary.

In the Larne area there are now five ordained women working in churches of various denominations, as well as several nuns. Ian's colleague is a woman, Frances Bach. It does lead to some confusion, but generally people have sorted out the various personalities. The women clergy in Larne do not meet together, nor do the Church of Ireland women have any formal group. Some would say we should, for mutual support, but perhaps it is good that we do not feel the need to, as we all minister in our own ways and bring our particular gifts to bear on our ministries. In the early days, when the media was anxious to talk to me, I was often asked what distinctive gifts I thought women would bring to the ordained Christian ministry. The question surprised me, and such a question still does, because I have always believed that every person, lay or ordained, male or female, brings his or her own individual gifts to ministry. I do realise that in certain situations I can relate better to women than a man could, but that is simply because I may have experienced a similar situation, illness or problem as the person to whom I minister. There will be occasions when a man can relate more readily to someone in a particular situation, simply because their life experience will help them. Each Christian brings to ministry something from life and something from their own experience of God. I am a mother, a wife and a priest. Therefore people automatically categorise me as being 'good with young people'. This is a gift I do not have. I am 'good' with young children, simply because my own children are young and I can work along the lines I would employ with them. Thus a junior choir of very small children, or a summer activity scheme for primary-aged youngsters, or a workshop on Good Friday, is something I enjoy doing, with a reasonable degree of success. Men too have their personal insights and thoughts, gifts and abilities; yet it is, in my experience, rare for people to categorise them.

It is thought by many that preaching comes easily to those who are ordained. I find this a particularly difficult thing to do well. Preaching in today's church – effective preaching – means knowing something about those to whom you preach and having something relevant to say to them. The community in Northern Ireland bears many scars, inflicted by a quarter of a century of terrorism and continuing low key activity by paramilitary organisations. For those of us whose lives were disrupted by the troubles during our formative years, but were otherwise untouched, it is hard to understand why so many people are so bitter. Perhaps this is partly why the reaction to my going to the Roman Catholic church in

Portadown was so strong. Many people in working-class areas are fearful about the future. They think that there is soon to be a United Ireland and that all Protestants will face extinction. But they also live in fear of members of their own community who, when the marching season comes around, demand money to buy flags and other political emblems which they erect on all available lamp posts and buildings. In addition to this fear, poverty and social problems are on the increase. For many, parenting skills have disappeared and young children roam the streets. When we preach we have to reach out, albeit indirectly, to these people, for the church has largely failed to get them involved. On the other hand, our preaching has to have a relevance for the middle-class people who cannot believe that social deprivation is a problem, or that during July people sit up all night to ensure their home is not the target of a petrol bomb. They bear a responsibility towards the working-class areas, and to making our church a welcoming place for them.

The Church of Ireland has long been proud of its pastoral care. Door to door visiting was the norm for generations of clergy, including my late father, who spent most of his ordained ministry in the Ballymacarret area of east Belfast: street after street of houses, no trees, no grass and dominated by the towering gantries of the Harland and Wolff shipyard. In those days – the late 1950s and 1960s – such parishes commanded a large staff of clergy. Nowadays the shortage of clergy and money means that most parishes are understaffed and the pattern of door to door visiting is very difficult to maintain. Priority must be given to certain groups: the sick, the bereaved, newly weds, those with specific problems, people with children to be baptised.

Recently, a young mother approached me about having her two children baptised. She is a regular churchgoer, divorced and living with the father of her children. She had received a rebuff from a male priest years ago who in the circumstances felt it inappropriate to baptise her children. Some would agree with his analysis, but in the Church of Ireland we cannot refuse to baptise those who live within our parish boundary. She was afraid to approach my male colleague and felt it easier to come to a woman. If the church is to be relevant to people and to show the love of Jesus, then we have to show care and compassion. And who can claim to be a follower of Jesus if they turn children away?

Sometimes the church and the clergy in particular are too concerned about what colleagues might think or what the congregation might say, so they do not take a stand. It is easier to say no than to receive a barrage of abuse. But sometimes we forget that Jesus did things which were considered inappropriate and even odd. We have continually to ask ourselves what he would have done given a particular situation. Another day and in a less than clean house, a 19-year-old with her second baby sat down to discuss having her children baptised. Conversation was difficult, as are her domestic circumstances, but she wants to do what she thinks is right. She wanted me to come to see her and to baptise her children because, as she told her granny, 'the woman minister was nice to me'. If I can be nice to these people and if they feel an affinity with me, then I think my ministry is worthwhile. Others of course would only want a man to deal with their pastoral care, but I think that increasingly men and women will and should work together to complement each other's ministries; and to give as much pastoral support and care as is necessary.

Despite the possibilities and benefits of women and men working together in this way, the Church of Ireland has not encouraged 'clergy couples' to minister in the same parishes. It was inevitable that there would be problems of deployment when couples were ordained, and some have had more problems in this area than others. Sometimes it means that one person has had to leave parochial ministry and go into another area to facilitate their spouse. A meeting of the various clergy couples with the Primate some time ago proved that there is a lot of anger with the way some couples have been treated. However, as time goes by and couples become integrated into the system, no doubt the problems will begin to ease. Besides, no one ever promised that being ordained would be easy. Despite being in almost constant contact with people, the life of the ordained minister can often be a lonely one. How many times have clergy officiated at funerals, particularly of people they barely knew, or perhaps did not know at all? How lonely those occasions can be, as family and friends share in grief and the minister tries to comfort strangers, or looks on as they comfort each other.

Perhaps one of the greatest problems for an ordained woman priest in the Church of Ireland, married to another priest, is that of the expectations parishioners have of the 'clergy wife'. This traditional role is largely disappearing as women have their own careers outside the home and beyond the church. Still, many expect the wife to run the Mother's Union branch, to arrange flowers and bake cakes. Whilst I do none of these things, there was still the expectation when we came to Larne that I would. It is strange that no one ever expects my husband to do what are perceived as masculine tasks in my parish!

Living in a Rectory brings all kinds of pressures to bear on a family. As anyone who lives in such a place knows, there can be times when the telephone rings constantly and people come and go frequently. There is the consequent necessity for confidentiality. Our children, young as they are, are being taught to respect that confidentiality and never to repeat what they might have overheard. Being a 'Rectory child' myself, I know that people expect the children to be extra good and extra spiritual. Michael, now seven, is a very reluctant churchgoer and a non-attender at Sunday school. When in church he usually finds a corner and immerses himself in whichever Roald Dahl book he is reading. Despite this, one of his classmates told her grandfather, a retired Presbyterian minister, that it wasn't fair: Michael Poulton knew absolutely everything there was to know about God because both his parents were ministers!

As a child growing up and as a raw undergraduate in 1980, I did not know what I would do, or where I would go. Writing at the end of 1997, I look back over seventeen years and wonder at how quickly they have passed and at what has been achieved. How did

I manage it? To have my name in a history book was never my motivation. To do what God called me to do was the driving force behind it all and continues to be. My personal aspirations at present are low key – to rear my family in a normal Christian family home and to minister to people in whatever ways I can. I hope that as I talk to children in school assembly, or walk through the estate to carry out pastoral visitation, people will know who I am and will understand that the church is there to reach out to them. I hope that when I preach in church, or teach a confirmation class, people will know I am proclaiming the Christian message. I hope the sick and bereaved will be comforted, not by me alone, but by God. And that all with whom I come into contact will know whose I am and whom I serve.

7   *This old hag, our Mother Church*

Georgina Baxendale

There can be few men who have had so many witty quips attributed to them as that old cynic W.C. Fields. He had made a living out of portraying misogynistic braggarts and cheats who often lay very close to his real character. Apparently he was typecast right to the end when he was spied leafing aimlessly through the Bible on his deathbed in 1946 and was asked what exactly he was doing. To this he replied sardonically, 'Just looking for loopholes.'

I have often found myself to be an unwilling participant in the journey of faith. At so many points on the road I have paused just long enough to look for loopholes. It was while living in Barcelona in Spain that I felt drawn towards the ministry. In those far-off days women were not exactly clamouring at the doors of the church. I suppose, then, that it was quite amazing that (unwilling though I continued to be throughout my training), these doors swung open for me. While I was busy scanning the fine print for loopholes I was somehow simultaneously hurled into the experience of my first parish in Coatbridge, in the sprawling industrial hinterland of west central Scotland. Looking back to my ordination, which was to Blairhill Dundyvan Parish Church, I am astounded at the courage shown by the folk there. Women in the ministry were commonly regarded as, at best, unknown commodities and objects of curiosity, and, at worst, highly suspect in their motives. And yet as a congregation they took me to their hearts just as much as I took them to mine. It was the people of Coatbridge who watched me and guided me and taught me to be a minister. Within a very short time I was ready to move on: first as associate chaplain to Glasgow University, and latterly as parish minister to Houston and Killellan. This united congregation has not caused me any real grief, since the union took place in 1771!

It is over twenty years since I trained for the ministry and in that time there have been significant changes. I am no longer described – with that hint of wry amusement mingled with curiosity – as 'the lady minister'. I can buy a clerical shirt which buttons to the girl's side. And, best of all, pregnant ministers are no longer given 'leave of absence on grounds of ill health' as I once was in the Presbytery of Hamilton. Indeed, we could be accused of 'having arrived'.

But, in all honesty, I have not felt at any point during my ministry that I 'had arrived'. I sometimes did not grasp which road I was on, far less whether I had taken the right direction. There have been tremendous highs and profound lows over the last seventeen years. During the high points I would not have swapped my ministry for the world. During the low points I longed for a real job which I could abandon at the end of a busy day and take up again the next morning. However, the one lesson I learned and learned early in the ministry was the stark fact that it would not be a life that could be easily abandoned.

When the difficult times have come, I remembered how wise my father was. He was not a man who could be termed 'Gospel greedy', and yet when I told him that I was going into the ministry he recounted something his father had told him. My grandfather had a plumbing business in Motherwell. My father was the youngest of a large family and obviously the apple of his mother's eye. She had high hopes for her boy. Her boy on the other hand wanted to be a plumber like his father and brothers. It was then that my grandfather gave his young son some very sound advice, which my father passed on to me. He was told that he had to think carefully about going into the business because 'it's easy to get overalls on but it's a hell of a job getting them back off'. And that, in effect, was what my father said to me about ministry. Yes, he would support me in every way, but while it would be easy to put a cassock on, it would be a hell of a job to get it back off. And so it has proved. On the rare occasions when the ministry did not live up to my expectations, or when I did not live up to my calling, I have always felt that I have been tied in to this extraordinary lifestyle.

I don't really know if the whole experience would have been quite as satisfying if I had been entering the parish ministry today. We have probably overcome most of the prejudices – and certainly the suspicions – which were directed towards women's ordination all those years ago. I suppose we have stood the test of time. Women have proved themselves and we are no longer news. When I recall the crazy questions which would now be classed as illegal that were put to us by vacancy committees, it seems like another world – a world of innocence, the charitable might say. It was entirely correct and proper that they voiced concerns about how women ministers would juggle the various responsibilities which emerge because of our gender. Such nuggets as 'Miss Naismith, what will you do if you get married?' 'How will you run a home and parish?' 'What would happen if you had a baby?' The shallowness of their questions was only to be matched by the shallowness of my answers. The point is that they were entirely the wrong questions, for no one can foresee the problems lying in wait in an individual ministry. The problems and challenges we confront have less to do with being a woman, and much more to do with being a human being trying to juggle the demands of the strangest job description imaginable.

If, seventeen years ago, a vacancy committee had asked me if I felt I would be capable of ministering to a congregation of nine hundred people, handling a broken marriage in the full glare of publicity, being a single parent, running a home and continuing to broadcast on a weekly basis for the B.B.C., I think I would have turned down the remit! But the questions that were asked of women were bland and trite, and showed no grasp of either the extent or the flexibility of women's capabilities under diverse personal or professional circumstances. They did not take into account how much an individual ordained minister is able to achieve with the support and love of a good congregation. And at the darkest time of my life I was lovingly surrounded and upheld by the community I served. The debt which I owe to the people of Houston cannot be repaid. They paid the full cost of ministry in the real sense by ministering to their minister when I needed it most, and, in so doing, taught me what it meant to be a part of the body of Christ in action.

We are now three decades down the line from the time when women were first ordained to the Church of Scotland ministry. The questions being asked have changed. This is in no small measure due to the fact that ministry has changed. There will still be the odd misguided vacancy committee who will discuss the merits of a minister based on their gender. There will, however, be a great number wanting to discuss whether a minister is 'successful' – whatever that means. This is a much more dangerous question! I remember shortly before my ordination I received a beautiful letter from Iain Muirhead (who taught me church history but who also had the dubious honour of having been my school chaplain). He offered me congratulations and wise words. He reminded me that I was not in the ministry to be a 'successful minister' but rather a 'faithful minister'. It is possible that God can do a lot more with faithfulness than with success, which is hostage to the whims of fashion. And from the dark recesses of my memory a verse of the Bible fails to spring to mind, but I do remember one story from the tales of Winnie the Pooh. Christopher Robin is about to knight Pooh. I think he uses the age-old command: 'Arise Sir Pooh de Bear, my good and faithful Knight' – or words to that effect. Now the point of the story was that the little bear realised that being good was awfully hard but maybe to remain faithful was the important thing. Perhaps he was right.

I suppose my experience of ministry has been marked less (for good or ill) by the fact that I am a woman, than by the highs and lows that have permeated my relationship with the church. I recently remarked to my sister that either Laura, my twelve-year-old daughter, was simply wonderful to me or else everything was wrong in our relationship. 'Oh, that's just adolescence – I remember it well!' she replied. 'Were you like that?' I enquired: 'No – you were!' she responded with a certain amount of smugness in her tone. And maybe that's where the problem lies: I am having an adolescent crisis about the church, which has now lasted for approximately twenty-two years.

Shortly before I was ordained, I was warned by Revd Jack Robertson, with whom I worked as a student, that the church was our Mother. Jack said, 'Sometimes you'll think of her as an old hag, but just remember she's always your Mother.' It was quite the most useful piece of advice I have ever received and I have often called these words to mind.

My ordination marked the beginning of my love/hate relationship with this Mother Church of ours. There has been so much in our relationship which has brought real joy. Her wit and wisdom, her loyalty and patience, and the sheer sense that she has allowed me to be part of it all. There has of course been the downside when I have despaired of the church's failings in different situations. There have been times when the hearts of her children have been broken through her apparent inability to reach out and touch the vulnerable, the dispossessed and the hopeless when they needed a mother's touch more than anything else. This has been a hard lesson for me to learn. There is a real paradox in believing that as ministers we serve a God whose voice was heard clearly in the desert; and a Christ whose voice cried out in agony from the cross. God's loving purpose was claimed in the desert and then on the cross. Yet so often we serve, and are part of, a church which regards deserts and crosses as too uncomfortable and risky.

Mother Teresa of Calcutta, like countless others, took on the risks of giving and service on behalf of the church and in the name of the God whom we serve. In her acceptance speech for the Nobel Peace Prize she stated quite simply,

> *When I was hungry you gave me to eat.*
> *When I was homeless you opened the doors.*
> *When I was weary you helped me find rest.*
> *When I was anxious you calmed all my fears.*
> *In a strange country you made me a home.*
> *Hurt in a battle you bound up my wounds.*
> *Searching for kindness you held out your hand.*
> *Mocked and insulted you carried my cross.*

> *When I was restless you listened and cared.*
> *When I was laughed at you stood by my side.*
> *When I was happy you shared in my joy.*

Over the years I have come to recognise that there is an unbearable tendency for the church to worry too much about what the rest of the world thinks. Maybe that comes from the policy-making bodies at the top! I'm sure, though, that the cream sneaks through from time to time – in spite of the power of ecclesiastical laws of gravity. It may be true that what the Church of Scotland requires is an accelerator rather than a moderator. Nevertheless, when big decisions have to be made, and the rest of the world may not be supporting our every move, the church has sometimes proved that she has good broad shoulders. Then she surprises us all by swimming against the tide, flying in the face of public opinion. Maybe it is only in such a church that women could have found the breadth of ministry in which so many of us have shared.

Too often the church is into 'bigness'. It is about power and control and accepting the world's standards of wealth and security and social acceptability. And this is a real problem for those who would take the message of the Galilean to heart. He stands for a total reversal of the world's standards. It is all about dying to live. It's about losing to win. It's about joy coming through pain. It's about victory through failure. It is about life through death. The institutional church can be guilty of paying homage to the superhuman, the superstrong, the superintelligent; the big, the bright and the shining. We are called, as the body of Christ, to use our humanity, our weakness and our vulnerability to embody God's strength in the world. We are called, and so often we fail miserably.

Given all of this, even when this Mother of ours is an old hag, she is still our mother. For the life of me, I have searched high and low, and even after seventeen years in the ministry I can't find an escape clause. However, that won't stop me from being on the lookout for loopholes!

8   *There are no women in abstract*

A reflection on the ministry of ordained women in
the Scottish Episcopal Church, 1978–1998

Alison Fuller

*By the tenor of these Presents, We, Richard, by Divine permission
Bishop of Edinburgh, Primus, do make known unto all, that on the
17th day of December, in the year of our Lord 1994, we the said
Bishop, solemnly administering Holy Orders under the protection of
the Almighty, in the Cathedral Church of St Mary, Edinburgh, did
admit unto the Holy Order of Priests according to the form and
manner prescribed and used by the Scottish Episcopal Church, our
well-beloved in Christ: ALISON JANE FULLER (of whose virtuous and
pious life, and competent learning, and knowledge in the Holy
Scriptures, We were well-assured; and she, the said ALISON JANE
FULLER, did then and there, rightly and canonically Ordain Priest;
she having first done all things which by law or usage are required
to be done preliminary thereto.*

So it was that I and my colleagues were ordained on that historic
day in Edinburgh. What was the journey which that led to that day?
What has it meant for our church? Was it all worthwhile?

The history of the Scottish Episcopal Church cannot exclude
reference to 'The Group for the Ministry of Women in the Scottish
Episcopal Church' which was formed in 1976. The story is told
about two women standing on opposite platforms at Haymarket
station. They had attended a meeting at Coates Hall – the residential training college for the SEC – at which GMWSEC leaflets had
been torn up, and discussion about women and ministry not
welcomed. One woman was absolutely fed up with the attitudes
expressed by those at the college, and soon after decided to leave
the church. The other went on to become the first woman to be

placed in charge of a congregation.

I began my ministry training at Coates Hall in October 1985. The original GMWSEC became the Movement for Whole Ministry (MWM), and my local group provided essential support and encouragement; because at that time I was the only residential woman candidate, and it was still not possible for women to be in Holy Orders.

In June 1986, the General Synod of the SEC passed the second canon enabling women to be ordained as deacons. The first women to be received into the diaconate were Di Forman, Janet Dyer, Elizabeth Malloch, Mary Pat Lennard, Mary Harrison and Patty Burgess. Almost all were MWM members, and had helped to shape our new aims, which were:

1. *To encourage laity to value and develop their gifts in service to the church and the world.*
2. *To assist the full co-operation of clergy and laity in exercising a whole ministry.*
3. *To support each other in the development of Christian education; particular support is needed by those who feel called to the ordained ministry.*
4. *To seek the development of a more inclusive and less gender-specific imagery, since we recognise that the language used in worship and theology greatly influences our ideas about God and humanity.*

MWM produced a new logo and established twice-yearly meetings: at Juliantide, and an Annual General Meeting in the autumn. The task of persuading the church to ordain its women priests was under way, and MWM was at the forefront of the struggle.

Janet Dyer was employed by the college on a part-time basis to be my tutor, and to provide a suitable pastoral placement as part of my training. But I also managed to do some work with 'Women Talking to Women', a local Community Education Group in the Gorgie/Dalry area of Edinburgh.

It was so important to have that involvement on my

placement, to counteract daily college life, where my voice was the only one singing an octave above all the rest at morning and evening prayers. There were occasions when I tried to wear my feminist colours on my sleeve: notably when I used inclusive language during the Office for Julian of Norwich. God our Mother was as much a problem for the male ordinands of the SEC in 1986 as it was for the General Assembly of the Church of Scotland in the same year (when the commissioners voted to 'depart from the matter' of discussing the report on the Motherhood of God).[1]

I completed my course in June 1987 and, after much head-shaking among the College of Bishops, I was appointed to a curacy in the Borders – working with not one but three rectors. It is time to acknowledge the debt we owe to those of all denominations who led the way in acceptance of women's ministry – often in forgotten rural areas, far from the centres of ecclesiastical bureaucracy and power.

In those first fragile months of being a newly ordained deacon, I was able to introduce myself as a woman minister whenever I visited people. To my growing pleasure, hardly an eye was batted. Later, once over the threshold and sipping tea with people in their homes, I would explain that I was a 'Piskie' – not the 'English Kirk' as we are affectionately known, but a member of the Scottish Episcopal Church. Certainly we were in communion with the Church of England, but ahead of them in the matter of ordaining women to Holy Orders.

I learnt so much from the good people of the Borders, even though I was never completely converted to the joys of Rugby Union or the pleasures of drinking whisky.

In June 1989 I moved to my second curacy at Holy Cross in North Edinburgh. These were also happy years, for I was serving in a more traditional parish, with just one priest supervising me. We established a warm respect and a long-lasting friendship – much, I suspect, to our mutual surprise. For me, there was something important about learning to work together as woman and man: complementing each other's gifts, seeing things from slightly different angles, interpreting the life of the parish, and sharing times of prayer and study. I believe that my priestly formation really began to have meaning in those times.

In the summer of 1989, the Synod passed a very interesting resolution entitled 'Women canonically ordained abroad'. This was a stop-gap motion which allowed women priests from other Anglican provinces to celebrate in Scotland, using their own rite. This allowed us to experience worship with a woman at the altar, and helped alleviate the hurt of those who had hoped that the motion enabling the ordination of women as priests would be passed that year.

It seemed clear to me that, for most people, the difficulties in accepting the possibility of female priests were to do with the novelty of the experience. I remember the first time I attended a Communion service at which the president was a Church of Scotland minister who was a woman. It had a powerful effect: that deep sense of seeing a woman's face reflecting something of the compassion of Jesus at the Institution Narrative. This is my Body, this is my Blood, do this in remembrance of me. My image of God was stretched that first time – enriched, enlarged, made whole.

In 1989, as a sign that there was growing recognition of the validity of women's ordained ministry, the College of Bishops issued guidelines for 'Deacons: Solemnisation of Marriage'. Concessions were made to allow deacons to dedicate or bless the rings; pronounce the nuptial blessing; and give the blessing of the couple and congregation at the end of the service. Ordained women were becoming more widely accepted and sought after – perhaps especially by those on the fringes of the church.

There were a few moments in my Borders ministry when my position as a deacon was brought home to me painfully and with force – for example, attending my POTTY training as it was affectionately known (the meeting of men, and myself, who were in our first three years of ministry). I was invited to the ordinations of many of my male colleagues, and these were special but sad times for me. It was something about learning the hidden blessings of the waiting time, especially as no one knew when that time would come to an end.

Then there were the times when I was taking Holy Communion to an old people's home, and there was no reserved sacrament left. So I would telephone round all the priests in the neighbourhood searching for a pair of 'Holy Hands' to consecrate more bread and wine. At other times, when because of sickness or emergency I was called upon to do 'Reserved Sacrament' services, I was told in no uncertain terms: 'Do not give the impression that you are blessing anything or anyone. Keep your hand firmly on the altar, and visible at all times.'

In 1990 I was invited by MWM to attend the ordinations in Belfast of Irene Templeton and Kathleen Young – the first women to be made priests in the British Isles. It was not only a great privilege to be there; it was also a stepping-stone on my own personal journey, for I was welcomed into Irene's family and parish. I learnt a little about what it meant to live in a religiously divided Belfast, and I saw the grace with which these two women were able to bear their part in the making of history.

The Church of Ireland followed the United States, Canada, New Zealand, Hong Kong, South Africa and Brazil as the seventh Anglican church to ordain women. It made clear to us in Scotland that, as a disestablished church, we had the freedom to lead the way, if we so chose.

It was with great sadness that I learnt a few years later that Irene had died of cancer, but it was lovely to have shared with her, Alan and Neil that historic weekend.

In July 1990, the Bishop of Edinburgh invited me to convene a meeting of all stipendiary women deacons working in Scotland. I believe that this was a recognition of the increasingly invidious position we were in. We had completed our first and second curacies, and believed ourselves called to be parish priests in a church which holds a catholic understanding of itself. The Reserved Sacrament service was not an acceptable alternative to Eucharist. What was the way forward, if actual priesting was not going to be possible in the foreseeable future?

In November 1990 we sent out a questionnaire to over forty women deacons of the SEC. The questions which concerned us were practical: What happens when a woman in full-time employment wants to start a family? Is there some sort of maternity leave? What happens when a non-stipendiary woman wants to become stipendiary? I believe now that these sorts of questions have wider implications for the management of church workers, but at the time they were emerging from a group of us for whom the church situation was provoking difficult issues. People responded with passion, and at a subsequent meeting a group of us drew up a document, 'Ordained Women Deacons in Active Ministry in the Scottish Episcopal Church', which stated:

Women deacons appreciate the complexity of the present situation arising from the suddenness with which it became possible for them to be ordained. There are now forty-seven women deacons working in five dioceses in the Province. Some are still in training, the majority carry substantial pastoral responsibility, including priestly duties. There is now enough evidence for the position to be clarified, and we make the following recommendations to the Bishops: i) That ordained men and women have a written working agreement; that there be non-negotiable, permissive and negotiable sections to this agreement (which will cover, for example, maternity and paternity leave) . . .

Team Working: many of our clergy have expected to work alone, but we recognise that there are lay people and other ordained people who are being called to work in a collaborative way. Team working as now understood is much more than having people of goodwill working together. It requires job analysis, well-defined areas of responsibility, and clear lines of accountability. It requires careful preparation in initial training and compulsory and appropriate in-service training; Career structure: We would like to hear the Bishops' suggestions for using the gifts and skills of experienced women deacons in senior positions in the Province (for example on Cathedral Chapters, as these are the main advisory boards to the Diocesan Bishops).

I quote from this report in detail because it highlights the far-reaching changes that those first ordinations set on course. Not only were we discovering what it meant for ourselves as women in the church, but I believe we were also asking the sorts of questions that ordained men had been wanting to ask of the church for some time.

On November 23 1991, I convened a meeting of ordained women in active ministry with two of the bishops. Reading through the notes brings back the intense feeling that we carried at that time. We, the ordained women, were a 'Problem', and the 'Problem' could only be solved by our ordination to the priesthood. We had long discussions about canons, and how to change them; bishops, and how to change them; sources of finance and how to increase them. Most striking was the reference to 'how we manage our anger'. For myself, the work of co-ordinating those ordained women who wanted to share their experience gave me a sense of not being so alone. It also reminded me that I was in an unusual position, as a full time deacon. (In fact at that time there were six of us across the whole of Scotland, out of almost 250 clergy).

It was clear to me even then that one of the ways we could take our 'Problem' forward would be to have a Woman Advisor to the Bishops and the Council of Ministry: someone whose paid remit would be concerned with the development of women's ministry in the province. But as a wise priest said to me, that would be the church putting its money where its mouth was. It still has not happened.

At least our meeting had prodded the bishops, and the following year the dioceses were encouraged to address the issue of women priests. In my personal journey, I had completed the three years of my second curacy, and although I had investigated working in New Zealand (because the idea of being under a woman bishop, Penny Jamieson of Dunedin, was extremely appealing) family circumstances dictated that I stay in Edinburgh. Much to my surprise, I applied and was chosen to be the Deacon-in-Charge at St Columba's by the Castle. At the time, it was said that St Columba's had always been a place that welcomed women's ministry. It was an awesome appointment and, looking back, if I had known the demands of the job I would have been rather less ecstatic. However, it was a calling and a response of faith – both for me and for the congregation that I have come to love over the past seven years.

In July 1992 the Church of England at its Synod narrowly defeated the proposal that women should be priested. Deeply disappointed by our sister church's vote, a small group of us met on the eve of the Feast of Mary Magdalen to formulate a strategy which would ensure that the legislation to allow women to be ordained go through the SEC smoothly.

MWM continued a campaign of producing educational pamphlets exploring the meaning of priesthood, from both an evangelical and a catholic perspective. These discussed issues to do with the 'headship' of women over men, with special reference to the Pauline epistles; and, at the other end of the theological spectrum, concerns about women 'representing' Christ at the altar. I believed that the discussion helped the church to examine more carefully the whole meaning of priesthood – for women and men, lay and ordained. But it was true that women were to some degree responsible for the modernising movement in the church. Bishop Michael Hare Duke, writing at the time, said, 'Women could bring a new dimension of leadership and vision to the contemporary church, providing they do not collude with existing expectations.' (*The Scotsman* October 1992)

By the time I gave my speech during the Diocesan Synod special debate, there were over 1300 female priests in the worldwide Anglican Communion. The case against women's ordination was put by my Coates Hall contemporary, Fr Timothy Cole. He was reported in the local press as saying:

> *We believe that women and men are equal in every way, but does that mean they must be interchangeable? The Priesthood is not like most jobs or professions – it is not about what someone does, it is about what they are and represent. Everything seems to point to God choosing men to be apostles, bishops and priests.*
> (Edinburgh Evening News, Oct 1992)

'Yes, Jesus was a man,' was my response. 'He was also Aramaic-speaking and a Jewish Galilean. Priests and bishops are none of these things.' (Evening News). The argument and image to which I returned again and again during these debating years was the struggle in South Africa for freedom from apartheid.

Certainly, we suffered to a much lesser degree. Yet the refusal to accept the vocation of women to the priesthood felt like a denial of our very humanity before God. Archbishop Desmond Tutu of Cape Town said:

> *The most radical act that can happen to any human being is to become a member of the body of Christ. If gender cannot be a bar to baptism, which makes us all representatives of Christ, and partakers of the only priesthood there is, his royal priesthood, then gender cannot be a bar to ordination.*[2]

On 17 June 1993, a vigil was held at St Columba's, organised by MWM. It was the eve of the first reading of the canon which would allow women to become priests. Sitting in the candlelight, towards the west end of the church, I remember watching an incredible cross-section of the church's membership come and go throughout the evening. There was a real sense that the Synod debate was surrounded by prayerful reflection. The House of Bishops and the House of Clergy gave well over the two-thirds majority needed. The House of Laity voted in favour by exactly two-thirds. It was an anxious time, and it indicated that there was still work to be done before June 1994.

I called a meeting of women deacons in November. By then we numbered over sixty. We explored the nature of vocation, and we tested the level of our morale. We spoke about our calling from God by name, of the need to know who we are, and to rest in our sense of inner freedom. This knowledge and comfort in our identity as women with a vocation to serve enabled us to minister to others in greater depth. But we also shared the frustration of the mechanics of dealing with the Reserved Sacrament; and we affirmed the need to remain hopeful that there would be a good outcome from the Synod vote.

During the first half of 1994 there were a number of events which encouraged us – not least the visit by Bishop Penny. She spoke at a conference in Edinburgh entitled 'Women Towards Priesthood'. We were reminded of some of the gifts which we as women bring to the church, and the 1989 legislation allowed Bishop Penny to celebrate in the cathedral, which was a source of great joy and encouragement.

MWM Juliantide meetings indicated their unswerving support for the cause. 'Wrestling with the Church' was Mary Levison's contribution in 1993; 'She who would valiant be' was led by Dorothy Peyton-Jones in 1994.

In my memory, the time of the June Synod is surrounded with tears: of pain and of joy. One member of 'The Living Church' (a group of traditionalists who opposed female ordination) handed over his precious copy of the Scottish Prayer Book to one of our women deacons, as a sign of goodwill: a brave and touching action remembered by many who were present. We also felt pain that there was to be a six-month 'cooling off' time before the actual ordinations. With hindsight, that was appropriate; at the time, we were so eager to proceed.

In July 1994, the women deacons met during the visit of Revd Ellen Aitken from the Diocese of Massachusetts. My notes from that occasion read:

We began by rearranging the furniture in that small room at St Mary's in order that we could sit in the round as opposed to around the table . . . Ellen reminded us that going forward to priesthood is not just about rearranging the furniture. It is appropriate that we should ask difficult questions. A priest is an icon of offering to God, and of offering God's goodness to the people; therefore a woman priest might offer what is at the margins; having struggled from the margins and from outside the centres of power, we might offer what the world has rejected.

It was at this meeting that I had the idea of encouraging the others to write down something of our experience as a 'Cairn on the Journey'. These writings were eventually collected and collated and form a 'family photograph album whose snapshots and occasional studio portraits bring to life the "Spirit of the Age" in a way no straight factual account could do'.[3]

So the days of ordination came. Across the province in December 1994, over forty of us women became priests in the Scottish Episcopal Church. For some church members, the pastoral sensitivity clause was insufficient and they left. Many others remained in membership, in the knowledge that no congregation would be forced to receive Holy Communion from a woman priest, if anyone was unhappy with the prospect. Our Primus, Bishop Richard Holloway, said during his sermon on that wonderful day:

> *The debate about the ordination of women in our Church has been a strange affair. On the one hand it has been a debate about theology, about the nature of authority, about women in the abstract. But there are no women in the abstract. There is only Elizabeth, and Jane, and Rosemary, and Alison, and Pamela – actual women with feelings and needs, longings and hopes, and they, many of them, have been deeply wounded by the years of struggle. Because it has been for them, not an interesting theological debate, not an exercise in ecclesiological reformation, but a felt injustice, a quite personal pain, an institutionalised rejection, an actual oppression. That is why many good women have lost their patience and left us. It is why Daphne Hampson now believes that Christianity and its God are intrinsically and incurably sexist – by definition misogynistic. This is a day of rejoicing and celebration, but we must not take it cheaply and easily in our stride. We must confess that for too long women have been wounded in the house of their friends and the whole Church has been limping in pain until this day.*[4]

Brave words, from a bishop who himself has travelled a long way to acknowledge the gifts and equality of women in the church. Gathered in the chapterhouse before the service, we were unsure whether there would be a demonstration or a legal challenge. Thankfully the only people with banners outside the cathedral doors were the Catholic Women's Ordination group, who had come to show their support.

I began by quoting the text which hangs now on my wall as a reminder of my priesthood. I also asked three questions:

> *What was the journey that led us to this day?*

I hope my recollections and archives of that journey shed some light and hope on the path of those who follow.

> *What has it meant for our church?*

I have hinted that I believe ordained women have helped the SEC to modernise, to look more carefully at the way it manages its people, to listen to those on the edge.

> *Was it worth it?*

Of course! To work as a priest in the church is a great joy. There are still those who find our ministry a novelty, and we have yet to debate the issue of women bishops. But no doubt that will come.

MWM publications

Susan M. Cole-King, *Julian for Today*, 1992

Donald M. MacKinnon, *The Icon Christi and Eucharistic Theology*, 1992

Ruth B. Edwards, *Christian Priesthood*, 2nd ed., 1992

Kenneth Mason, *The Catholic Tradition and the Ordination of Women*, 1993

Stuart George Hall, *Authority in the Church*, 1994

Rosemary Nixon, *The Priority of Perfection: Genesis 1 and 2, and the 'Order of Creation'*, 1994

Trevor Hart, *Evangelicals and the Ordination of Women*, 1994

Valerie Shaw, *Elizabeth Malloch: An Ordained Life*, 1995

Alison J. Fuller, *Cairns on the Journey*, 1997

Notes and References

1   This report, written by Dr Alan Lewis of New College (who was secretary of the Assembly-appointed study group), was one response to the outcry when Anne Hepburn, National President of the Church of Scotland Woman's Guild, opened one national Guild Meeting with a prayer to 'God our Mother'.

2   Source unknown.

3   Foreword, *Cairns on the Journey*, MWM, 1997.

4   Sermon preached by Bishop Richard Holloway, December 17 1994, at St Mary's Cathedral, Edinburgh.

9   *Paths are made by those who walk in them*

Joanna Anderson

There is a saying which I believe comes from the Native North American tradition. It holds a great deal of meaning for me: 'Paths are made by those who walk in them.'

I was born in Liverpool in the early 1950s, the fifth child of six in the family of a Church of England clergyman and his wife. From the rough and run down dockland area of Toxteth, I moved, as a toddler, to the wide open isolated spaces of marshland Essex.

Most of my childhood playtime was spent alone in the rich pastures of my own imagination. But, far from feeling isolated, I had, as a child, a strong sense of belonging to the natural world, and of it and myself all being closely held in the arms of God. Here is a powerful memory from that time which says it all.

High summer in my sixth or seventh year, I was alone in a wheatfield (in the days when it felt safe for one's children to be off alone playing). I was lying back in the field, under a dazzling sun in a clear azure sky. Above me hung the heavy golden ears of wheat, and bright scarlet poppy flowers crowded among the stalks, gashing the field with pools of their brilliant presence. I was gazing into the clear sky, intent on pinning down the source of a torrent of sweet song pouring from a skylark somewhere high above me.

In the song, in the vibrant heat, in the gold and the scarlet of the field, in the deep cavern of sky above me and down in the centre of my being I knew that all was well. I had a clear, unquestioning awareness of the Creator, the goodness of creation, my part in it and the whole thing pulsing with the presence of living love.

A potent memory of childhood faith.

That was not something I held for long; indeed it was soon to be knocked out of me by the passage of time and several overcast and unhappy events in my life, including the death of my mother while I was still a child. Yet that experience of certainty set me off, all those years ago, along an unending path of searching for that grounded, incarnated faith at the heart of Christianity.

On that path I have often been the first one to walk. In my family, I was the first and only child to go into higher education. Having for the most part disliked the experience of school, I had found that religious studies did grab my attention, so I followed through to take a theology degree at a Scottish university. Not a hugely academic pupil, I found far deeper satisfaction in the many performances I got involved in with the drama society. For my studies, it was only by the grace of God that I obtained a degree, because I was more often than not to be found falling asleep in the back row at a lecture.

The theological degree did not lead me into the church. Indeed those studies put me firmly outside the church for several years. Far from academic theology enlivening and deepening my faith, it contrived to stultify such beliefs as I had in my late teens and early twenties and to convince me of the irrelevance of the church and her creeds to my life, which was, during my twenties, a time of turbulence and turmoil. I spent the most part of the next six years going down dead-end streets and taking wrong turnings that led me up blind alleys. However, the start of the 1980s set me on a new path, which eventually put me back onto the track of a living faith.

I came into contact with members of the Iona Community for the first time, and found in them women and men who were living out a radical, earthed faith in their daily lives. Here were people who were attempting to exemplify the Beatitudes in ordinary lives: for instance, by living among and alongside the poorest people in Scotland's cities, or else by being non-violent peacemakers on the frontline at Greenham Common and other places. Here too were people who spoke of a God who is intimately involved in the created order and who requires humanity to join in the endless task of being co-creators. Amongst these people was the Community's founder, George MacLeod. Like so many before me, I was deeply inspired by his presence, his challenging words and his patent faith in a God of justice, mercy and incarnated love in the world.

I went to work for a time on the island of Iona, at the centres which are the Community's shop window for its rule, and became a member in 1982. During these years, I was not breaking new ground but I was discovering that the threads of my experience were all clearly leading me to one point. When I left Iona in 1984 (along with my husband whom I had met and married there), I returned to England – intent on taking a route into the Church of England as an ordained person. From this point onwards, I experienced the reality, in my own life, that 'paths are made by those who walk in them'.

I trained for ministry in the Diocese of Lincoln, and because I had been away from the Church of England for several years, the Diocese was initially reluctant to sponsor my training. I went to selection school and was asked to return a year later for a review. By this time I had two children, the youngest of whom was a few weeks old, and I believe I was one of the first women to go to a selection board review with a baby at her breast. I did think to myself at the time, during this most searching of processes, that if they would take me on for ordination training – bared breast and all – then there was hope yet for the Church of England. And they did!

I was ordained a deacon in 1988 and went to be the first woman curate in a parish in an urban priority area of the steel town Scunthorpe. Yet another untrodden path.

However, this town, with its long history of welcoming and integrating migrant workforces from parts of the world as disparate as Bangladesh and Ireland, was an easy place to settle into. The congregations never once made me feel out of place or unwanted in my ministry because of my gender. Indeed they were chuffed to be the first parish in the diocese to have a pregnant curate. This was another path waiting to be made: for the diocese had never, until I came along, been faced with pregnant clergy and their need for maternity leave. We helped the diocese put its final policy into place.

Life as a deacon and curate and mother of three very small children was often exhausting but filled with challenges. One of these was to give our children a stable home life, knowing myself how strained life in clergy families can be. We tried employing live-in carers. Although they were delightful and great with the children, they kept leaving after a few months to get married. The alarm bells rang for Peter and me when our oldest child asked us, 'And when is Mummy leaving?' One of us had to relinquish full-time salaried employment. It turned out to be my husband, who has always been the staunchest supporter of my move into ordained ministry. He gave up a very well paid job in industry to be the anchor person at home, taking on all aspects of housekeeping and child care. In this he too was forging a path, for in industrial South Humberside men who could command salaries like his did not opt for the kitchen sink unless they were made redundant. Peter has continued in this role for nine years so far.

After a curacy of four years it was decision time. The Church of England had still not, at that point, made up its mind to ordain women to the priesthood, so the prospect of moving into a more responsible job or of broadening my experience in the church was very limited. We looked to move. And the move brought yet another unexplored path my way.

I was appointed as the first Anglican Warden of Iona Abbey in 1992 – a post described by one of my fellow community members as the most difficult job in the church. Not only was I the first Anglican to hold this ecumenical post, but I was the first ordained Anglican woman to hold it. I walked along that particular glorious and agonising path for three years. As I recall that time, and that appointment, it was a tremendous privilege, but also one of the most isolated and lonely periods in my ministry. This was so for two main reasons.

Firstly, I came to the post ordained as a deacon in my own church – well trained both sacramentally and pastorally to be a deacon. However, the diaconate order of ministry is so little recognised in the wider church that within the liturgical practice of the ecumenical worship at Iona Abbey, with its strong emphasis on lay leadership and involvement, there was no place for this particular role. Non-Anglican members of the Abbey staff, and of the wider Iona Community, had no understanding of the office and work of a deacon in Anglicanism, and I found that I had to put a very important part of my ministry on ice for almost three years.

The other aspect that saddened me from the start of my time as warden was the way in which quite a number of people, both within the Iona Community and outside it, expected me to break with my orders and do things on Iona which at that time I was not permitted to do in my own denomination. This principally meant that there were people who expected I would consecrate the elements at a communion service.

The sanctuary of Iona Abbey has a very long history of welcoming and encouraging different denominations of the Christian church to share in the worship within its walls. (Indeed, openness to all Christian traditions was one of the conditions set by the Duke of Argyll when the Abbey church was restored 1901–10.) But I believe that it cannot continue if those who oversee the worship of the Abbey itself do not respect the integrity of each denomination.

As warden I knew this and felt strongly that I should not disobey the rules of my denomination, but rather stay within my orders as a deacon of the Church of England. Therefore I never consecrated the Holy Communion before my priesting. During the first three years as Abbey Warden, I continued, like my sisters of the Anglican Communion in England, Wales and Scotland, as a deacon in relation to the Lord's Supper. For me this brought a deep sadness. I would welcome groups of people to stay on Iona. I would work with and walk alongside staff from all over the world. I would lead group work with people, touching some of their deepest experiences of life. I would listen as a counsellor, pray with those who asked, bless marriages and baptise babies. I would strive with others to weave community among people through the weeks and months. And yet, when we came to the feast at the heart of our faith – the Eucharist – I could not stand at the Lord's table and invite my sisters and brothers to share the sacrament from my hands.

Through all that time I did not feel that this was ever understood – even by fellow community members. So the pain was as much to do with isolation as my personal situation.

When the vote finally went through – in England first, and then in Scotland – I had to wait longer than most, because I had ended up in an Episcopal diocese where there was a small but very powerful body of resistance against the ordination of women to the priesthood

I was, however, ordained priest in January 1995, in Oban Cathedral, and the last six months on Iona as warden were deeply enriched for me.

In 1995 the latest pathway came into view for me. As I walk along it, I discover there are indeed new ways to tread.

I am now the rector of seven parishes in the Norfolk Broads. A deeply rural area, set in rich farmland, it is peopled still by many families who trace their lines back for generations in this very area. Time and again I come across an elderly person who lives in the house where she, her parents and even her grandparents were all born. I am glad that it was relatively easy for my three children to make the transition to such a settled and rural environment. The two older children transferred from a one-teacher school with nine other pupils, on Iona, to a Norfolk school with two teachers and forty pupils. My youngest child has begun school here and is already well on the way to a local accent. For us as a family, Norfolk is a good place to be while the children are growing up, although like all other country dwellers we often have to travel many miles in the car with them to get to piano lessons or scouts.

As the first woman priest in these parts I have once again been warmly welcomed. This strikes me quite forcefully, because I would characterise these marsh people as pretty deeply conservative in their views and behaviour. Yet they unanimously chose a woman from a selection of contenders for the job, and in doing so broke new ground.

As a female incumbent, I realise that my style of leadership is very different from that of my male predecessors. My tendency is to work with and alongside my congregations, discovering first who they are and how they tick. The prevailing model for those clergy in charge of parishes is to get in quick with your own agenda, make changes from your point of view and expect the parishioners to come along with you. I have been far more a leader who consults, listens and negotiates with people to get things done. I realise, too, that I understand power in a way which is, perhaps, rather different from the perspective of my male colleagues. For me, power is conferred by my role and position. The folk in my parishes have been used to the rector simply telling them what will happen. His word has been law. My way is to share, discuss, confer – always with the hope that we might find consensus (though in practice this is rare).

I also have an approach to worship which is much more concerned with enabling all those who belong to the worshipping community to participate according to their own level and gifts. I seek to make sacraments, scripture, preaching and prayer as accessible as possible to everyone. I bring a very personal approach to preaching, concerned always to connect scripture with people's ordinary lives and experience. My understanding and practice of ministry may be shaped by gender, but perhaps it has developed just because I am who I am.

An interesting sidelight on my gender is Peter's position as the rector's husband. In the past, the rector's wife was clearly pegged as unpaid curate, ever ready to open her home to the parish and to pitch in on parish teas, flower rotas, running a fete stall or whatever was needed. Many clergy wives of the last twenty years have broken this mould. It has been a relief for them to be released from playing a stereotyped role, so that they can simply be themselves. Most clergy families can barely survive on the stipend alone. The necessity to earn money, as well as the personal satisfaction of career development, is gradually making the ever-available 'rector's wife' obsolete.

My husband Peter came to these parishes wondering how he would be regarded. In fact, there has never once been a 'clergy spouse' expectation laid upon him in the parishes: which quite surprises us, given the conservative nature of the area and its love of tradition. Clearly these good Norfolk folk are not to be pigeon-holed or second-guessed!

'Paths are made by those who walk in them.' These words continue to hold so much truth for my life as an ordained woman. I am always turning unexpected corners and discovering new things along the way. Recently I preached in our diocesan cathedral and my sermon seems to have made a strong impact on several people, not least because I preached in a way and a tone that apparently is most unusual in that cathedral. But I realise also that it was a surprise (a pleasant one, I trust) for many at that evensong to see and hear a woman speak loudly, clearly and with authority in the mother church of the diocese. It was new for them; it was unexpected too.

I return to Iona to set the seal on this part of my journey so far, because whatever path I find myself travelling along – even when I am on it as a token woman (as I am on some committees) – I rejoice to be there. I sense the continuing privilege of this life, despite its stresses and strains for myself and my family, and I look forward (as we pray in the daily office of the Iona Community) to find 'new ways to touch the hearts of all'.

10 Snapshots on a journey

Viv Lassetter

It is very difficult to write about oneself. As I think back over my life and calling, I realise that I do not think tidily. I recall events in flashes and jerks. These bursts of memory are like pictures in an album, so I have called them snapshots. I share them hesitantly because they are special times in my life. As I wrote down the pictures, I realised how many snapshots are caught in candlelight. This was not deliberate and I chose not to edit them. Candles are a part of me, as those who know me well would testify. My home is full of candles which I light on every occasion and none. When she comes to stay, Imogen my three-year-old granddaughter expects to eat her breakfast by candlelight. Well, why not?

I come from an Irish Roman Catholic family. A family of storytellers, a family of strong feisty women who have lived hard and sometimes sorrow-filled lives and who have yet none the less never failed to see the funny side of life and faith. When I am with my mother and her sisters, I realise how much like them I am. They accept me, and my ministry, and do not remonstrate with me for choosing a path that is different to theirs. Last time I was with them and they were shrieking with laughter over a situation in which one had found herself, I suddenly thought of Jesus sitting down to dinner with Mary, Joanna, Salome and the other women who journeyed with him. I know he would have enjoyed the earthy humour of my aunts, and I realise that in the last ten years I have come to a greater appreciation of the company of women as I have grown to be at ease with myself and have come to understand my intrinsic worth to God. This too has been part of my journeying.

One of the most evocative scents for me is the scent given off by a smoking candle. I always want to waft the trailing mist of smoke towards my nostrils before breathing in deeply. Even as I write I am reminded of a snapshot framed in time with its own special smell. It is a candlelit Kairos moment.

Snapshot one

I am seven years old and am standing before a statue of Our Lady who is dressed as always in blue; hands clasped, praying intently, eyes fixed on the unseen things of heaven. All around her are penny candles of varying lengths, flames flickering in the draught, casting a shimmering comforting glow over those who stop to light and pray. The candles are visible transient signs of moments of faith, hope and thanksgiving. I am about to make my first confession. I light my candle and pray to become a saint like Bernadette who at fourteen had a vision. I hope I won't have to wait as long. It is a big prayer for one so young but my candle, tall and splendid, says it all. I believe in God and God believes in me.

This particular snapshot is located in the last decade before Vatican Two. I was a restless questioning child, chafing against the restraints placed upon me because of my gender. Why did boys have all the fun? Why did Desmond get to ring the little bell at Mass? He was as naughty at school as I was. At least I knew my Catechism. I longed to dress up and swing the incense but, alas, it was never to be. I longed to be special and when confirmed chose the saint name Bernadette whose story never failed to move and inspire me. I toyed with the idea of a missionary life but knew that with my fear of spiders I would be very limited as to where I could serve.

Snapshot two

I am around ten years old, and am upstairs at a friend's house. We have made a den and are eating a picnic inside. Suddenly my friend's mother shouts up the stairs that we must come down at once. Surprised, we clatter down the stairs and into the living room.

Her parents are sitting down looking very serious. The Pope is dead. Pope John XXIII is dead. I feel very strange. It is almost like losing a distant grandfather. What will everybody do now? My friend's mother makes us all a cup of tea and I go home.

I was too young to understand the implications of Vatican Two. Too caught up in my own small trials and tribulations to appreciate the pain that comes with change.

In my early teens I developed an interest in music and singing. On Sunday evenings I would watch *Songs of Praise* and can remember my fascination with the 'Singing Churches' that featured week by week. At my church there was no music. We didn't sing at all.

Snapshot three

Another candle glow picture. It is almost midnight on Christmas Eve. This is the most special time of year for me. I am at church, a Baptist church, packed into a pew with about a dozen young people and we are singing a well-loved carol. I am seventeen. There are no statues here. The candles are in tidy brass candlestick rows on the windowsills all around the church. These candles will not be allowed to wilt and slither all the way down to the floor. These candles will not stay lit long enough to smell as candles should. They will be snuffed out just after midnight and put away for another year. None the less they cast a rosy red glow upon the wooden pews and brickwork and I am glad of them.

I had met these young people at a coffee bar run by the local Baptist church. I had been accosted by two scruffy lads giving out invitations on a crisp clear evening. Free coffee, the invitation said. Just what I needed. So with two friends alongside for moral support I entered a non-Catholic church for the very first time. I attended the coffee bar and then the youth club for quite some time before agreeing to go to a church service. One evening, however, curiosity got the better of me and I went to church. There was not a great deal to see. Very little colour; the focal point was a plain cross. There was nothing to smell – no incense or candles. But there was singing! It was a 'Singing Church' like those on *Songs of Praise.* I decided to stay.

I got married in a Baptist church and had both of my daughters dedicated. Settling into motherhood, I attended church regularly, and as the girls grew I took on more responsibility, becoming a house group leader and deacon.

Snapshot four

I am sitting in a hall at an interdenominational conference. Along with several hundred others I am listening as a man explains the meaning of the story of Samson and Delilah. Samson had allowed himself to be tricked by a treacherous woman who had used her natural wiles to lull him into a false security. Poor Samson. Bad Delilah! Suddenly I am intensely aware that I am being spoken to deep down in my spirit. I feel some words being pressed within and upon me. 'I want you to feed my sheep and tend my lambs.' Had God spoken to me in the middle of a sermon about Delilah? If so, what superb timing! I look about me. Nobody has noticed my surprise. The man on the platform is still speaking. I sit quietly and remember my seven-year-old self and my desire to serve God. I am married now with two small children. Can I really have heard correctly? I decide to wait and see. I believe in God – how much does God believe in me?

I was not completely sure what the 'call' I had felt at the conference actually meant. I was active at my church where women were encouraged to participate fully, although there were no female elders. My church was lively, fast growing and involved in church planting. Every now and then groups of leaders from other churches would come to teach and encourage us. It was always good to meet with people who were a step ahead.

Snapshot five

A group of leaders have come to church. I know them well and am relaxed with them. It is the last day of their visit, almost time to say goodbye and we are gathered together for the last few moments before we must reluctantly see them off. Suddenly one of them turns and says to me, 'Do the words "I want you to tend my lambs and feed my sheep" mean anything to you?' Only Maureen, my closest friend, knows of the mystical moment at the conference. We glance at one another. I decide that it definitely was God who spoke to me. Where will I go from here?

I am fortunate in that the church I attended was pastored by a secure leader. He was delighted for me on hearing of my call and said that I must be given the opportunity to preach. He also gave me books to read about women in leadership and introduced me to Feminist Theology. It is a scary business to test a call. It is much safer to hug it to oneself and keep it, precious, private, unspoken. God, however, calls things into the light and so I eventually followed the testing process which for me included going to theological college.

I had never set out to become a Baptist, never mind a Baptist minister! I had gone along to a Baptist church first of all because I liked the singing. There was no agonising theological thought process involved. At the local Baptist church there was singing and there was a large group of very friendly young people. These two factors settled the matter for me. When I then married one of these young people, I believed my future path was laid out.

Not everyone was thrilled by the latest developments in my life. Some friends found the idea of women ministers very difficult to come to terms with. Not all Baptists think alike on this subject. This was a difficult time for me. This call was so much a part of me that rejection of it could not easily be separated from rejection of me. Would these friendships survive?

Snapshot six

It is Advent, my first Advent at college. I cannot remember ever marking the beginning of Advent like this. We are all gathered together, the whole college community, in church. On the floor at the front somebody has sketched in chalk the outline of a human being. The lights are very low. We are singing a simple chant. All of us are holding night lights, and tapers are passing among us to kindle the little flames into being. All of the night lights are lit. The lights above are extinguished. We sit in church, shadowy figures singing by candlelight. Then we begin to flow down the steps into the aisle, still singing as we place our lights on the human being who represents Christ the Coming One, but also we ourselves who are in Christ. As I place my vulnerable little light on the edge of the figure, I am suddenly elated. I am glad I am a woman, not just glad, but thrilled. I watch my little light for a moment. I do not want it to go out. It is a sign: my symbol for this Advent moment that God believes in women and so believes in me.

College was a breath of fresh air. At college I was surrounded by grown-ups who *didn't* want to stop growing. It was a place of affirmation, of struggle and a great deal of laughter. At college I learned of the Risk Taker God, the God of birth pangs; the God who lures with love and who never gives up on us. At college I met afresh with the Incarnate God who washed dirt-encrusted feet and came first to a woman with the greatest news of all. At college I learned to be vulnerable, I learned how to challenge and to accept being challenged as I entered into the joys and frustrations of trying to build community. I knew within a very short time of arriving there that I would be changed for ever. At college I encountered passionate people who were fierce in their desire to see justice walk with faith. I learned the meaning of solidarity and listened to those who would come and explain the wild helplessness that is experienced by all who are oppressed and marginalised.

In college I would browse for hours in the library and nobody complained that I was wasting time. My understanding broadened and God grew! I believe that my college experience helped my spirituality to deepen. I learned how to use language inclusively, rediscovered liturgy rhythms and seasons, and began to experience the healing peace of silence. At college a love of music was reawakened along with a latent gift for creativity. At times I felt as though I was being put together like a jigsaw puzzle.

Snapshot seven

It is our last day at college. My year group and I have become very close friends. On this day we have chosen to celebrate a silent communion together. We invite a tutor who has been involved with most of our small group moments to share with us.

A silent communion is very dramatic. Because there are no words we must keep eye contact. Nobody can hide. This is demanding, and requires a group who are secure together and sure of one another. We have celebrated together like this two or three times before. This last time at college is etched in my memory for ever. We are on the threshold of ministry, these friends and I. What will the future hold for us? At the end of the liturgy we stand in a silent circle and bless one another. Nobody must be left out. For four years we have worked, laughed, cried and prayed together. We have held each other up, and cheered each other on. Now we must let go and test who we are and what we have become. How can we bear to part? Suddenly the tension is broken as the youngest member of the group blesses our tutor with a large bowl of water. We all join in the water fight, then, remembering that the room will soon be needed, we rush to fetch towels.

Nobody who enters a Baptist training college to train as a minister can presume that at the end of training their future is assured. After training there must come a call from a local church. Only then can one embark on the next stage of the journey.

In August 1992 a call came from a church in Lancashire asking me to be their minister. I accepted and planned an ordination service to be held at my home church. This service further alienated the friend who was struggling to accept my vocation. I made the painful decision not to pursue the relationship, but to allow my friend to set the pace and make contact as and when she felt she could. This had been a close friendship and the cost to all concerned was dear.

It was time to look ahead, to decide how best to serve this church which had shown trust and confidence in me. I had served my college apprenticeship, had worked as a student minister with two churches, and now it was time to put all I had learned into practice. At this time I was greatly helped in my thinking about worship by Eleanor Kreider; she and her husband Alan were Theologians in Residence at college. Eleanor's book written about worshipping congregations, *Enter His Gates*,[1] also stimulated my thinking in this area.

The church asked me to pay particular attention to children, young people and worship. As a church we wanted to draw the younger ones in, helping them to feel a part of things, and thereby instilling within them a very real sense of belonging. In order to do this I needed to get to know each child and young person individually. This was no hardship, as these youngsters were responsive, curious and friendly. They more than met me half way.

During my training I had thought a great deal about worship. I wanted to experiment with colour and memory association. For instance, the smell of candle smoke flashes my memory back to childhood and the day I was to make my first confession. Many North Americans associate well-being with the smell of freshly roasted coffee and home made apple pie. I wondered if learning about God and the church could be made easier by such association.

Snapshot eight

It is the first Holy Week after my arrival at Sion. It is six-thirty in the evening and sixty-five people are crammed into an upstairs room waiting expectantly. We are about to hold a form of Passover Supper in remembrance of the Last Supper Jesus held with his friends.

I am seated with the children, the youngest of whom asks the gathered assembly, 'Why is tonight different from all other nights?' I tell the story of the flight from slavery and the parting of the Red Sea. I recount how all through the years Jewish people have come together at Passover to give thanks for the unfailing love and providence of God. Later on during the evening I will remind the people that the Last Supper Jesus shared with his friends was a Passover meal eaten on the night he was betrayed.

After the Bible reading I take a taper and, after giving thanks, ask people to light the candle in front of them and pass the taper to the person on their right with a word of welcome and blessing. Gradually all the candles are lit and the children sit enthralled as the room comes to life and the food is brought in. We eat roast lamb and I hope that in the years to come this taste and smell will remind them of this special night and our reason for being together. After the meal we clear away the plates and tables, and through song and dance celebrate the faithfulness and providential love of God. Tomorrow will be Maundy Thursday, the start of our solemn services as we move from an ecumenical communion service to Good Friday and on into the celebratory worship of Easter day. As the evening draws to a close several youngsters are already clamouring to do it all again.

One of the chief joys during my time at Sion was to sing with the choir. I love the camaraderie of singing with a choir. I gained a great deal from the choir of Sion Baptist Church. They were newly formed when I arrived, but over the next few years we built up our repertoire and also managed to have a lot of fun. The choir attracted a wide age range – the youngest member was sixteen, the eldest in his eighties. They were willing to sing a very wide range of music so that in any one service we could sing traditional hymns, choral music and choruses, which the choir would lead with aplomb. Introducing new songs was so easy. We would learn on Thursday and teach on Sunday, and we worked hard to include something for all age groups.

In time some of the children expressed a desire to sing. We formed a youth choir and twelve young people aged from eight to fifteen came together. The senior choir watched with deep satisfaction as these young ones grew together in confidence and began to produce some stunning music.

During the Spring of 1997 I was offered and accepted a denominational post. Almost as soon as I knew for sure that I would be leaving, the grieving process began. I wondered how I could possibly leave these people. I realise that such thoughts invariably accompany a big decision, but I was unprepared for what turned out to be a physically and emotionally draining experience. From the moment I told the church I would be going every event took on a new and poignant significance.

I had been so very fortunate to have been called to a church who appreciated what I had to offer; even when they were unsure of something they were willing to give it a try. Some people found change difficult but understood the need to move on and let go of things that had outlived their purpose. I felt loved and respected and this in turn strengthened my confidence. My congregation looked to me to give a lead but I was never left unsupported. We worked collaboratively. One elderly man said to me not long after I came, 'I understand now what you meant when you said you were an enabler. You meant *we'd* do it!' He was smiling when he said it and he was almost right. But 'we' always included 'me'.

In May we held a creative arts day to prepare for Pentecost. An artist had joined the congregation and I asked her to use her skills and resources to help us decorate the church. A group of adults and children duly arrived wearing old clothes and baggy shirts. We covered the hall floor in newspapers. Anita, our resident artist, had provided us with large sheets of paper, paints, string, acrylics, glue and other materials. To start the session off, I asked the children what they thought about when they thought of Pentecost, and they answered, 'Wind, fire, breath and water.' 'The colour red,' said another child. Just before my first Pentecost Sunday at the church I had suggested to the congregation that we all came wearing something red, the colour of fire and festivity. We then turned to our paints and paper to make our own creations. It was messy and fun. I suggested that we do it again for Advent. 'You won't be here,' said a small voice accusingly.

After lunch we produced a large banner on stretch canvas and a painting for every window in the church. The acrylic paint made them translucent and they looked very effective. We painted jam and coffee jars and placed candles inside them. When all our efforts were dry we carried everything through and decorated the church. It looked magnificent. On Sunday the people came wearing red as usual and the children opened worship with a song during which they twirled sticks with long red ribbons attached. It was a feast of colour and celebration. It was my last Pentecost with them and one I shall never forget.

Because I had been asked to broaden worship I worked hard to introduce the church to a variety of styles and experiences. A number of people had expressed interest in contemplative worship so we purchased songbooks from the Taizé community and organised a monthly evening service. A small group gathered month by month to sing these simple but profound songs and to learn how to use silence effectively.

From the beginning three, sometimes four, younger teenagers would come early to help me set out the candles. They liked me to put them out and light them in a particular order and often brought a candle of their own to add to the growing collection. When the service started they would sit on the floor and could usually be relied upon to behave well, even during the long silence. One of the proudest moments in my ministry was on hearing after I had left the church that two of these young people, only thirteen years old, had by themselves arranged and led a Taizé-style evening which was greatly appreciated by the adults who attended.

It had been some time since I had had any real contact with the friend who had been unable to accept the ministry of women.

Snapshot ten

I am working in the kitchen, preparing dinner. I feel a little low as an afternoon spent at the church has highlighted the struggle some are having in coming to terms with my leaving them. As I mull over the problem the phone rings and Anne tells me that she is really looking forward to seeing me soon. I am a little nonplussed and turn off the dinner in order to give her my full attention. Why would she be really pleased to see me? She wants a long chat sometime. A great deal has happened since we last spoke and her thinking on women in leadership has changed. The intervening years roll away; we are chatting again like the close friends we used to be. I promise to go and stay, bringing books and photographs. After much laughter we hang up. I feel better. Blow dinner! I make a cup of tea and go off to hunt out the books she has asked for. This is a moment of celebration and jubilation and I am going to enjoy it!

Snapshot eleven

It is my last day and the whole community of Sion have gathered together in the church hall. We have eaten a feast, a 'Jacob's Join', as they call it in Lancashire. Afterwards we sit together at small tables to watch a farewell concert which has been organised in secret behind my back. I have since forgiven them their duplicity and the subterfuge for which they have a remarkable talent. Everybody has contributed something to the proceedings and people have been practising various acts. The choir and youth choir sing songs of their own composition and present me with photographs. Alex, a church member and former choir leader, has written a hymn especially for me. This is Sion at their very best. When the concert is over we troop into church and I lead my final service. I arrive home exhausted and feeling emotionally drained. An unopened letter falls out of my handbag. It is from Amy who is sixteen. She writes, 'When I am your age I hope I am like you, only taller. You have taught me to be a woman of faith and I will never forget you.' I will never forget her either.

I have never regretted going into the ministry. I still feel called and although my new post has taken me out of the local church I am still a Baptist minister with opportunities to preach and pastor. My vocation has not changed. The girl of seven has journeyed a great distance since the day of her first Confession. I knew nothing about women ministers; I had never met one. My journey has been one of discovery, both about God and about myself. At times it has been a surprising journey, often scary, always exciting. Looking back to the call at that interdenominational conference I wonder, if I had known then what the future would hold, would I have had the courage to pursue God's call? I am grateful for the support and encouragement of my family and friends and other women students and ministers who have shared their lives with me.

Notes and references

1   *Enter His Gates,* Eleanor Kreider. Marshall-Pickering, London, 1989

11   *Claudia's sisters*

Lesley Carroll

It is difficult to know where to begin when telling a story. What should I leave in and what should I leave out? What are the really important things? I have had to live again some steps on my journey. It isn't easy to open up some of the old wounds and find that they aren't so well healed as I had hoped. Not all the hurt has been because of my gender and not all the joy has come because I am a woman.

It is interesting to reflect on the fact that at different times in my life I would have felt a different focus appropriate for this article. I was ordained in 1988 and proceeded to finish my training as ordained assistant in a large Belfast congregation. I then moved to an inner-city parish in Belfast where, as they say, I had the time of my life. Almost seven years later I now find myself 'unemployed', minister without portfolio if you like, and looking for a new parish.

Transitions have never been easy for me. That is partly due to my nature and partly due to knowing somewhere in the back of my mind that the issue of my being a woman limits my choices, induces feelings of being invisible and in some senses devalues the work I have managed to do. It certainly doesn't help when people acknowledge this limitation of choice and describe it in trite ways as if it didn't really matter too much. As one man said to me lately, 'Yes, it is awkward.'

Many men respond by arguing that their choices too are limited. While this is true, one would also want to say that such limitation in opportunity is due not to gender but to choices those men have made. In other words, they have some control over the limitations in their lives and experience; I do not. Those who judge me on grounds of gender alone devalue my work and try to steal from me and from the church the gifts with which God has blessed me.

From time to time I wonder if I shall ever escape the dilemmas and the ceaseless questioning. I wonder if I shall always have the strength and courage to stick with it. I wonder if I shall be able to hold true to my vulnerability and not disguise it but find God through it. I hope these aren't bitter reflections, but I am human. I know that bitterness destroys the self, erodes relationships and cramps possibility. This is the first challenge – not to become embittered or brutalised by experience but to be re-created by it, to be re-created in God's way. And through it all to be able to hope and dream. In the words of an Australian Aboriginal proverb, *'Those who lose dreaming are lost.'*

As I look back over the years, my time training in Belfast comes immediately to mind. Those years can only be described as the wilderness years. It was like living in a pressurised bubble, a microcosm of the hot issues of church life. As a single person I was required to live in college accommodation but there weren't the facilities for a woman to live in the same building as the men. So I lived in a flat across the road with a gas heater for company.

I naively thought that friendship could conquer difference. I enjoyed the company of the other students and I appreciated any opportunity for discussion and debate. We met every week to study and pray and as our three years ended we looked forward to ordination and to supporting one another in the years ahead. But then the crunch came.

A few months before we were to be ordained we met as usual to discover that some of the men in the group felt they could not continue to meet with the women after ordination. If we did meet together, they said, then we simply couldn't talk about anything to do with ministry. I was hurt, dismayed and deeply disappointed. These were people with whom I had spent the last three years of my life. I had invested time and energy into making these relationships work. I had lived with the need to be respected for who I was and I thought I had managed it. But clearly who I was, what I had been or hoped to be, the kind of friendship I could offer – these things didn't matter. And it certainly didn't seem to matter that I was, like them, going to be moving out into an uncertain world without the support of those whom I thought had become my friends.

It all seemed so ludicrous anyway. Ministry isn't something I do during certain hours of the day. Ministry permeates every aspect of my life. There is no way I can avoid talking about it in any relationship that is remotely meaningful. I was being asked to deny myself and I was being asked to deny my calling. I and the other women in the group felt we could not continue to meet under these terms and so we simply left them to it.

Looking back I wonder why we didn't set up a group of our own. The ordained women do meet together but those of us who withdrew that day never tried to set up an alternative group. I suppose that would have been to deny something of our belief that we have to learn to live together, with all our differences. Alternative groups are not the answer but a way of buying into the already failed pattern of separating ourselves from those with whom we don't agree. Despite it all I still prefer to choose the naivety of friendship as a means to overcome difference. This is the second challenge – to remain committed to the whole church and not opt for alternatives which, in the end, will face the same problems and probably make the same mistakes.

The language of the church too is difficult to bear. The Code of Practice for the Presbyterian Church in Ireland is couched almost entirely in male language. When we have asked for a revision to more inclusive language we have again and again been pointed to the hours of labour this would take. Time is clearly more important than people. Hymns remain exclusive when they need not be. Even in meetings where many women are present, there are men who address the assembled group as 'men'. The challenge is how to bring such matters to attention and explain their importance, while learning to live with the silent scorn and cool reception

To exist inside this church is sometimes to exist with out-and-out rudeness. But perhaps that is not the most difficult thing to bear. Perhaps what is most difficult of all is living in the experience of being rendered invisible. Being treated as a non-person, pushed away, not spoken to or prayed with – this is not the Gospel. God didn't choose to push us away and write us off because we were different. God chose our company. God chose the price of keeping company with those who were different. There is a price for us all in life and in the choices we make. The question is whether or not it is a Gospel price.

Jesus once went to dine at the home of an important man, a Pharisee named Simon. Every preparation would have been made, carefully planned to the last detail. What was not planned was the unexpected arrival of a woman. As a woman she wasn't welcome to sit at table, but her lifestyle made her doubly unwelcome. However, without fuss and without words but with deep devotion she took out her small flask of myrrh. Having washed Jesus' feet with her tears and dried them with her hair, she anointed his feet with the sweet-smelling, expensive perfume.

Simon (and, no doubt, his other guests gathered at table that day) was horrified. The look on their faces was probably enough. They wanted rid of her. They wanted to render her invisible. But Jesus would not allow it.

> *She has done what she could; . . . Truly I tell you, wherever the good news is proclaimed in the whole world, what she has done will be told in remembrance of her.* Mark 14:8-9

This challenge comes to me unexpectedly but it is welcome nonetheless. It is the challenge to remember that while there are those who clamour to render me invisible, God does not. I need not live hiding, frightened, isolated. I need only live in the presence of Christ who sees, knows and understands faith.

Now so conscious of difference with members of my own denomination, I find myself asking question after question. Questions about how we engage difference, how we transform conflict. Questions about truth and where it is to be found. Questions about how I should relate to those who don't want to relate to me. Questions about unforgiveness and unrepentance. How am I to respond?

I do not ask anyone to believe exactly what I believe. I cannot do so. I am looking for space for myself. I cannot deny others that space for themselves. Each person has the right to make their own decisions and choices. I can dialogue with others but to put pressure on them to change is simply to operate, from the other end, the same model: 'I know the truth and I will persuade or browbeat you until you believe the truth too.' I have the deepest of respect for those who value who I am and what I do and yet maintain their right to have a different opinion to mine.

How am I to respond? What kind of response should I aim for, knowing full well that many times I will miss the target?

Everyone should be quick to listen, slow to speak, and slow to be angry. For human anger does not promote God's justice. James 1:19b–20

That is not to say, of course, that anger should always be avoided. We, like Jesus, do find ourselves at times overwhelmed by anger, but for it always to be our first resort would serve no good purpose. I have been angry for years and now that it has begun to dissipate I can see how it binds and traps. But I don't want to forget the anger or be deprived of the capacity to be moved by it. Both memory and experience of anger direct me to a sense of fairness and give me energy to work for something better. However, directing anger at another person with the intention of hurting them as they have hurt me achieves nothing but a spiral of destruction.

My friends, you believe in our Lord Jesus Christ who reigns in glory and you must always be impartial. James 2:1

Growing up in a mainly Catholic Nationalist part of Co. Tyrone as a member of the Protestant Unionist community, I have seen the devastating effects of mismanaging difference. I remember feeling different on the bus to school – three of us Protestants among a whole busload of Catholics. There was an inexplicable, irrational but very real fear of being different. And there seemed to be no way of genuinely facing the difference.

I belonged to an enthusiastic Youth Group in our small, closely knit Presbyterian congregation. Like most young people we were interested in many questions and the time inevitably came when we asked questions about Catholics – What did they believe? Could they be Christians? We thought that the best way to have our questions addressed was to speak with a Catholic and so we asked if we might invite a priest to come to one of our meetings. We were told that this was not possible as it would give credence to the Catholic Church.

It seemed that to be different from us was to be without value, and indeed lack of respect of this kind has cashed out in the horrendous cost of violence in Northern Ireland. It has led to Protestants murdering and maiming Catholics and Catholics murdering and maiming Protestants. Politics and religion are all mixed up and so some of those who espouse Protestantism and Unionism have found justification for putting down the other community and some have found the impetus to kill and maim. It works both ways. Nationalists and Catholics are no better and no worse.

In May 1974 a Catholic woman whom I knew well was driving home with her husband after work. They were civilians, friendly and obliging people. They had been in our home just a week before. As they drove up the lane to their home, gunmen from the Ulster Volunteer Force (a Loyalist paramilitary organisation) mowed them down. Gertie and Jim left three children. Their only crime was to be different, on the other side.

A young man had just set up a gardening business. It all seemed to be going well, coming together at last. He was a Protestant, a member of the Ulster Defence Regiment. He worked in our garden at home. In 1988, aged twenty-three, John was shot in his car by the Irish Republican Army. His only crime was to be different, on the other side.

This is just a part of the record of the careless desolation and plunder of life in and around one small village. Similar stories could be told across Northern Ireland. Is this any way to live? What alternative model does the church offer for dealing with difference? Do we show how much we value life, even the lives of those who are different? The churches would not advocate murder nor condone it but in our own way we have contributed to supporting a model that makes murder and mayhem possible.

This is the next challenge – to find models for handling difference, models which value and respect life. And when I encounter situations in which I am devalued, overlooked or even openly dismissed, to hold true to this alternative way that is based in acceptance, grace and the celebration of difference as an impulse to creativity, hope and a better future.

Thankfully there are two sides to every story and so, alongside the dilemmas, struggles, hurts, hopes and fears, there are also resounding positives. I struggle to keep them in my mind and to be continually affirmed by them.

For the past six and a half years I have been working in inner-city Belfast in a community where the stark differences which exist for people in Northern Ireland are clearly seen in peace lines, graffiti and what has come to be known as recreational rioting. The people found in this community, with whom I have been privileged to be, are the church. They may not know how the church structures work. They are not to be found in meetings where important decisions are taken; they are not the kind of people whose opinions are sought; but they are the church. If you ever find yourself asking where God is to be found, I can assure you that among such as these I have seen and met the Lord who is to be found among the hungry, naked, poor and imprisoned.

I am sustained by these people who inhabit the fringes of society. They have not only welcomed me as their pastor but also joyfully pastored me. They are part of an alienated and divided community. It is a community where unemployment is high and skills for employment are low. It is a community where para-militaries exercise control, houses are bricked up and few people are interested in continuing education. We live between walls which keep us apart from those who are different from us. These walls, along with metal grilles which protect windows and empty streets after dark, are summed up in a piece of graffiti found on one of the walls – WARSAW 2.

The church building which I call home straddles one of Belfast's peace lines. The peace line is a fortified fence to keep Catholic and Protestant, Unionist and Nationalist, apart. During the day gates along the line are open but there are few who cross to see the streets and homes on the other side. Our building can no longer claim beauty but the people can boast grace. Light is no longer permitted to stream into the building, for windows are boarded up, but among the people you will find reason for the light of hope. Draughts from around the buckled window frames do not impair the warmth of loving acceptance. I am sustained by this community. I am sustained by their faith, hope and love in the face of adversity. I am sustained by single mothers who, with dignity and honesty, struggle to bring up their children; by those who have been robbed of their loved ones by Northern Ireland's troubles and yet refuse to be unforgiving; by those who have lived a life of violence but who now work every hour God sends to bring understanding and harmony to divided peoples; by those who chose the paramilitaries and yet are prepared to listen and consider another way; by those sexually abused, some by leaders in the church, who will not turn away from God and do not walk away from the church because they believe the church belongs to God and not to those who dehumanise and degrade others; by alcoholics, prostitutes, those who are gay, prisoners, the elderly, the confused, the hard-working, the frightened, the lonely. Among all of these, these least of our society, I have met and been challenged by Jesus Christ.

It has been my privilege to administer the sacraments, bury the dead, visit the sick and share people's lives in the context of inner-city Belfast. To be afforded the honour of holding a newborn baby and blessing it in the name of the triune God has been my single person's part in the family, in the future. To invite people to come and sit down at the Lord's table where they will be fed and welcomed has been enhanced by seeing those who thought they weren't good enough to come receive the invitation and share. To sit with the dying in the long night hours and weep with their families has allowed me to glimpse the world to come where there will be no more death, no more parting and no more sorrow. To struggle to interpret the Word to people whom I know and whose situation I know has been joy, privilege and boundless opportunity. I could go on. Suffice to say that I have been ministered to by those on the fringes who have afforded me the space to be their pastor. Among the powerless, by those rendered invisible by society, the church and political confrontation I have discovered the meaning and mystery of friendship.

I also found welcome among my colleagues of every tradition. We meet regularly to talk, pray and reflect. Catholics and Protestants: together we are called by God's Spirit to live the Kingdom in our own particular situation. For a number of years I have been a member of the Inter-church Group on Faith and Politics. It is sponsored by the Irish Council of Churches. This group of people from different traditions, and both parts of Ireland, comes together to reflect, from a theological point of view, on the political situation. This has been both challenging and rewarding. Membership of this group has made me aware of all the various influences in society.

It seems to me that the churches tend to make one of two mistakes. Either we see ourselves as so important that we don't have to talk to anyone else, or we see ourselves as having so little influence that we don't see any value in engaging others. To that end our local clergy group has been meeting political representatives, community leaders, the Royal Ulster Constabulary and anyone else who is willing to talk. It is our agenda to listen and recognise that while different groups in society may not begin from the same position or operate out of the same motives, we are all united in our commitment to a better society. In these meetings I have been encouraged by the welcome and challenged by the views of others. I believe these are important meetings, for all of us share responsibility for the society in which we live.

I am sustained too by other ordained women – by their stories, indomitable hope and indestructible commitment. These women of today stand alongside the women of the Bible to encourage, challenge, guide and support. These women, like Sarah and Hagar, have been victims of patriarchy, but give clues about living in a system which is opposed to equality. Among this company of women there are those abused by men: women like Dinah and Tamar. And still there are those devastated by such abuse and crying out for justice and a society that will honour them.

Intelligence and courage too mark the lives of these women: women like Rahab and Abigail. Others, like Vashti and Esther, although defined by their powerful men, found ways boldly to refuse exploitation and stand for justice. This crowd of women, clustered throughout the years of history, includes devoted mothers like Jochebed and Hannah, leaders and prophets like Miriam and Priscilla, faithful widows like Anna and Dorcas. They are women touched by Christ and by the life of Christ. They are women who are, and have been, privileged to be witnesses to the resurrection. They are women who, like the unnamed wife of Pilate, seek to speak out in the most difficult of situations. Their names may not be recorded and few may remember them. Thankfully some do: in the Greek Orthodox tradition Pilate's wife has been canonised as St Claudia and a feast day, October 27th, set aside for her.

Named or unnamed, remembered or forgotten, these women and their faithfulness are known to God. Those on the edges with stories of exclusion, alienation and powerlessness – these too are known to God, the God who hears and values their stories. It appears that the church has not the same wisdom to listen.

But that too is unfair, for there are those who have listened and have encouraged. They have been people of both traditions – Catholic and Protestant. Over the years when Catholics have listened and assured me of their prayers I have wondered where the Protestants are who profess to know the truth. Where is the loving presence of Christ through them? Why do some want to cut themselves off from sisters and brothers and deny themselves the joy of a shared journey? And so I turn to a new stage of life, to studying ecumenical theology and learning of the broader Christian heritage.

Like Claudia, like named and unnamed women in every generation, like all those who inhabit the fringes of society, I am known to God. I am known by name and my story is heard. When I come near to God in the press of the large crowd who clamour for God's attention, l can be sure that I will be seen and heard and understood.

So after all I find that the experience of being marginalised is not an experience of death but of the reality of life – life full of joy and hope and challenge. The church may turn a blind eye, and often refuses to listen. If it does decide to listen, it often will not hear. This is the refusal of life. It is the institutional church so deeply involved in writing its own epitaph that it can no longer truly see life and live in God's future.

For the creative potential is realised in dialogue. It is realised when we see our theological formulations as nothing more than theological formulations. God alone is the truth. Creative potential is realised too when we understand ourselves to be in dialogue with the text of Scripture and its authors, and we need the insights of dialogues from other contexts and situations. The God I have met is found in Belfast, in the inner city. The God you have met is to be found wherever you are. But this God of whom I speak is not the fullness of God – only a tiny drop. I need you and you need me to discover more of the truth about God. Dialogue is life and hope and possibility. In dialogue we shape one another as stones bumping against one another by the ocean's edge. In dialogue we walk and talk guided by the Spirit of God who gives us ears to hear and eyes to see and hearts to understand. In all of this we are not strangers to God but friends of God. As the psalmist wrote of God,

You trace my journeying and my resting-places, and are familiar with all the paths I take. Psalm 139:3

This is the beginning of hope, the hope that has sustained people through the centuries. This hope is heard every time someone speaks out against the dominant voice of the crowd – just as Claudia did. This speaking out is faithfulness to the gospel and faithfulness to Jesus Christ. Claudia has indeed many sisters. We know some of their names but, like Claudia herself, they go largely unnamed. Nevertheless, they are those who believe in the future and remain faithful to it.

Acts of faith bring life and hope. Like the man who risked all and didn't bury his talent in the ground, so women in every generation have lived prepared to take risks. For these risks they have been rewarded and entrusted with more.

12   The waiting time

Helen Blackburn

I was born into an ordinary Catholic family in the north-east of England on October 23 1965. I was to be the eldest of four daughters. Some of my earliest childhood memories are of chaotic Sunday mornings, as my Mam and Dad got us all up, dressed and into the car in time to get to church for 8 am Mass. We always sat near the front so we could see what was going on. Somehow we didn't see the priests as 'ordinary people'. I grew up in a Redemptorist parish and in those days it was very unusual not to see the priests dressed in their distinctive black habits. After Mass we would go to visit my Gran and Grandad and sometimes we would play 'Mass', improvising with an assortment of tea towels and pigeon-racing trophies! It was never disrespectful: it was rather that being part of the church and going to Mass every Sunday was a significant part of our childhood. On reflection I sometimes wonder how my parents managed. I'm sure we must have been late occasionally!

I went to the Catholic primary school, next door to the church. I think I probably enjoyed most of my time there. I didn't understand the term 'gender issues' then; I just knew that there were some things that weren't quite right. I couldn't understand why the boys and girls had to play in separate yards when we could all play together in the street at home. Or why, when we had a film show or party and there were desks and chairs to be moved, it was always the boys who were asked to help. Things didn't get any better when we made our first Holy Communion. The boys looked smart in their shirts and ties, but I couldn't understand why the girls had to look like mini-brides in their veils and frilly white dresses. I don't look terribly happy in the photograph, but it wasn't something you'd have dared to protest about at that time. When we learned about the sacraments, we were told that there were seven . . . but that the girls could only receive six. No one attempted to explain why, and the girls were left feeling marginalised and excluded.

On Wednesday afternoons, the entire school would go round to church for Benediction. This was the real thing, mostly in Latin – at least until I was well into junior school. Of course, what with all the candles, the bells and the incense, there were a lot of altar servers needed. Once the boys in my class started to be altar servers, I could hold my peace no longer and I asked if I could be an 'altar girl'. I was told in no uncertain terms that this was not allowed, but I could give out the hymn books instead. Again, no one ever made any attempt to explain why. Later on, the argument was put forward that altar boys were potential vocations to the priesthood, and having girls serving alongside them might put them off! Eventually, in April 1994, the Vatican agreed that it was acceptable to have female altar servers, but only if there were no men or boys available! Of course many parishes had had female altar servers for years so this was not such a big issue for them, but for me it was a significant turning point. It showed me that the hierarchy was beginning to acknowledge the diversity of women's ministry. It is very interesting that when lay people were commissioned as Eucharistic ministers over ten years ago, both women and men were asked to take on this ministry, which involves actually administering the consecrated elements of Holy Communion. Yet women and girls had to wait several more years before they could simply assist the priest through the ministry of serving.

It would be all too easy to feel quite negative about the apparent lack of progress made in promoting and developing women's ministry, but it is important to keep a sense of historical perspective. I am too young to remember the Latin Mass said by the priest with his back to the people, with minimal participation from the laity; too young to remember Mass without lay people serving as readers. Mass in the vernacular with lots of participation seems perfectly normal to me because it is what I have grown up with. For many others, change is difficult to cope with, and they

often long for things to go back to the way they were. I recall my
Gran saying that she did not think women should read at Mass, but
that was over twenty years ago, and perhaps it was something that
her generation would have become used to and accepted as a valid
ministry for women.

In 1976 Pope Paul VI published *Inter Insignores*, and I vividly
remember the headline in one of the Catholic newspapers: 'Vatican
says no to women priests.' Of course it did not encourage the
faithful to engage in dialogue – it simply said no. I must have been
about ten years old. I didn't understand why, and yet again no one
wanted to explain why. The idea that I might have a vocation to
ordained ministry hadn't really crossed my mind then – probably
because I knew it wasn't possible. But I was starting to give the
issues surrounding women's ordination some fairly serious thought.

The rest of the world was starting to think about women's
ordination too. Who can forget Una Kroll's cry from the gallery –
'We asked for bread and you gave us a stone' – when the Church
of England General Synod voted unsuccessfully on women's
ordination in 1978. In the United States of America, the Roman
Catholic 'Women's Ordination Conference' came into being in 1975
but it must have been another ten years before I found out it even
existed, and some more years after that before I found out how to
join. Meanwhile, nearer to home in the late 1980s I had visited an
Anglican church. I cannot remember which church or why I was
there . . . but among a pile of literature on a table near the door
was a leaflet about the Movement for the Ordination of Women
(MOW). This was a real gift! I took the leaflet home and joined
MOW immediately. All of a sudden I had access to literature,
information, booklists, newsletters – and t-shirts! I still have my
MOW t-shirt, although it's getting a bit old and faded now. I was
really proud to be a member of the Movement and even took part
in an overnight vigil outside Lambeth Palace. My sister was highly
amused at spotting me on Breakfast Television! I met Myra Poole
for the first time at that vigil. She was to be a founding member of
'Catholic Women's Ordination' some years later.

In the meantime I had survived school and an assortment of part-time jobs before I did my training as a psychiatric nurse. Around this time I continued to go to Mass every Sunday and also took a more active role in the parish. The issue of female altar servers was still there for me, but I had volunteered to be a reader and was asked to be among the first group of Eucharistic ministers commissioned for the parish. I was also asked to represent young people on the parish council. Not everyone appreciated my strong viewpoints, particularly on women's ordination, but I responded by making sure I did a lot of reading around the subject and kept myself well informed about developments. We had a very active local Council of Churches (now known as 'Churches Together'), and there were opportunities to participate in ecumenical events and visit other local churches. I particularly enjoyed visiting churches where women were active members of the ministry team. I still make time in my busy schedule to visit other churches from time to time and feel that we cannot place enough importance on the work of the ecumenical movement. For me ecumenism is about trying to understand rather than trying to change; about recognising diversity whilst promoting dialogue.

I wish I could have been there in Dean's Yard on November 11 1992, when it was announced that the Church of England General Synod had voted in favour of ordaining women to the priesthood. However, I was several thousand miles away sweltering in the heat of a college in Lusaka, Zambia, where I was working as a VSO volunteer. I had taken my short-wave radio into work with me, and was at my desk listening anxiously when the results came through on the BBC World Service. I was delighted for my Anglican sisters, but couldn't help feeling a bit sad that we as Roman Catholics still had to wait.

People at home thought of me and it was fun to receive so many British newspapers. The tabloids excelled themselves with headlines such as 'Vicars in Knickers', but thankfully my dad had the presence of mind to send a wonderful cartoon from *The Guardian* which occupied pride of place on the wall of my house in Lusaka for the next eighteen months. It was about this time that

I had been thinking seriously about my future. I was enjoying my work in Zambia but could not, and did not want to, stay for ever. I had applied to a number of universities, received some offers, and eventually decided to go to Edinburgh, because it appeared to have a particularly good Department of Christian Ethics and Practical Theology. The Anglican women would soon be ordained, but some of us had a long wait ahead of us. I decided the waiting time would be put to good use. I had written some years earlier to a wonderful Roman Catholic priest, Fr John Wijngaards, after reading his book: *Did Christ Rule Out Women Priests?* He wrote back to me and said that we must believe that women's ordination will come, and he said it was important to prepare myself academically if I felt that ordained ministry could be my calling. I took his words very much to heart at the time, and thought about them as I accepted the offer from Edinburgh to read for a Bachelor of Divinity degree.

Catholic Women's Ordination (CWO) was officially launched on March 24 1993. I missed out on the launch as I was still in Zambia, but I became a member and was determined to get involved as soon as possible. I moved to Edinburgh in October 1994 to start my degree, and one of the first items of mail I received was a CWO newsletter. In it was an item about the Edinburgh group, along with some dates and addresses for meetings. I had obviously made the right decision to come to Edinburgh! As it happened I was able to get involved at a very exciting time. Earlier that year the Scottish Episcopal Church had voted to ordain women to the priesthood and the first ordinations were scheduled to take place in December. Obviously CWO wanted to give these women our support, and I actually got involved with the group as they were planning their activities for the day. The ordinations in Edinburgh were to take place on December 17 1994.There were to be fifteen women and two men, and, as it happens, the only candidate I knew was one of the men!

Our plan was that we should have a short service of prayers and readings outside St Mary's R.C. Cathedral before processing to St Mary's Episcopal Cathedral. Everything went according to plan, even though one of the clergy outside the Catholic cathedral told us in no uncertain terms to get our banners away from 'his property'. We duly moved the banners, continued our service and processed to the Episcopal cathedral where we could not have received a warmer welcome. The Very Reverend Graham Forbes, Provost of the cathedral, came outside to welcome us, and was even happy to pose for a photograph! We had expected to remain outside during the service, but the Provost ensured that seats were found for us. I had a lump in my throat throughout what was really a very moving ceremony. I don't often recommend watching 'the video' of anything, but in this case I certainly would. I could have listened to Bishop Richard Holloway's wonderful sermon over and over again. The press did not ignore us and we got some really encouraging publicity. It was a marvellous day and we were fired with enthusiasm to do something similar on a regular basis.

Some of the CWO groups in England had started to hold monthly vigils outside their diocesan cathedrals, and we felt this was something we could also do. We chose Thursdays (late night shopping in Edinburgh – more people around), set Thursday June 1 1995 as the date for our first vigil, and issued a press release. A multitude of reporters, photographers and late night shoppers turned up to watch us get absolutely drenched as the heavens opened for one of the heaviest showers Edinburgh had seen in months. However it didn't dampen our enthusiasm (no pun intended!) and on the first Thursday of every month, even if it falls on New Year's Day, we continue to hold our vigils, remembering named and unnamed women who have contributed to the church and the world over the centuries. These have ranged from Mary Magdalene to Mary Seacole. We wear something purple to symbolise our mourning for women's lost and rejected gifts. We sing, we pray, we keep silent and we think of our foremothers who have been such an inspiration to us. It's not always easy to keep the vigils going, especially during the summer months when people are on holiday, but we always seem to manage. Once a year, on the Tuesday of Holy Week, we hold a special vigil to coincide with the Chrism Mass during which the holy oils to be used over the coming year are blessed and distributed, and the clergy of the archdiocese renew their promises of ordination.

The campaign does bring its challenges. I have been writing letters to the Catholic press for many years: not just about women's ordination, but on other related issues such as ecumenism and inclusive language. For my troubles I have received in the post a number of anonymous letters – not always polite – along with an assortment of 'right-wing' journals. I don't know whether reading these publications is meant to convert me. Being fairly open-minded I would probably read them if the senders had the courage to say who they are.

For some reason, those opposed to women's ordination often seem to think it is perfectly acceptable to be rude to people like myself. I have had people who barely know me demand to know what kind of books I read and whether I go to Mass. Even priests have made unpleasant jokes at my expense. One or two have even asked me why I don't just become an Anglican. At the Chrism Mass last year, I was handing out leaflets to people entering the cathedral. I offered one to a woman who took it, ripped it in half and almost flung it back at me. She was so angry, but the incident made me feel sad. I put the torn pieces into my pocket and kept them for several days. I just couldn't stop wondering what it is about the issue of women's ordination that brings out so much emotion in people. Does ripping a leaflet in half make someone feel better? Is it fear of change, fear of the unknown, fear of what the hierarchy might think? I don't have any answers but I do think a ban on discussion contributes significantly to the problem. Surely it would have been far more helpful if the Vatican had said it did not feel the time was right for women's ordination at the moment, but that it is important to keep discussing the issues, the ethics and the theology.

CWO is one of many organisations throughout the world campaigning for women's ordination to Roman Catholic priesthood, but the issue is wider than just that of ordaining women. We need to acknowledge the importance of all ministry. As a child I thought that being an altar server was 'more important' than giving out the hymn books. I no longer allow myself to be conditioned into thinking in such a way. In fact I would argue that we are all called to some form of ministry within the church. This may be the ordained ministry of priest or deacon, or it may be the ministry of making the coffee after Mass. We have become very good at creating hierarchies within ministry instead of acknowledging the unique and special gifts we each have to offer. The most valuable gifts any priest or minister possesses are those of encouraging, enabling and affirming all members of the church regardless of their particular calling. I often think of elderly people who are no longer able to get to church, yet pray every day for the parish and all its members. If that is not ministry then I don't know what is.

There are different forms of ministry which clearly belong to the historical tradition of the Christian church. At Easter 1996 a conference was held in Stuttgart entitled: 'The diaconate: an office for women in the Church? An office which does justice to women?' The conference resolution asked the bishops to seek canonical permission from Rome to allow them to ordain women as deacons within their dioceses. The call for women to be admitted to the diaconate is certainly growing and it is one that CWO actively supports. Those who feel called to this kind of ministry have been asked to join the International Network for the Diaconate which is based in Germany.

CWO is a small (but growing) organisation with a huge remit. We believe it is important to achieve a forum for examining, challenging and developing the present understanding of priest-hood. For me, this certainly means supporting the International Network for the Diaconate. It also means supporting other forms of ministry, campaigns for inclusive language, and the ecumenical movement. Here in Scotland, CWO has become involved with the Network of Ecumenical Women in Scotland (NEWS), which is a committee of ACTS (Action of Churches Together in Scotland). The committee comprises representatives from each of the ten member churches of ACTS, along with those of several co-opted groups. CWO applied to become a co-opted group, and most of the NEWS membership welcomed our application, but there were those within ACTS who challenged the validity of our organisation. The matter was discussed at length by people in high places before we were eventually offered observer status. Naturally, we were disappointed that obstructions prevented us from joining our sisters on an equal basis, but we know that observer status is a start. We are grateful that NEWS and ACTS acknowledge and respect us as an organisation.

Closer links have also been forged with the Movement for Whole Ministry in the Scottish Episcopal Church (MWM). The women and men who belong to MWM have been through a similar struggle, and we really value their friendship and support. It is also very important that CWO members throughout Scotland are able to keep in touch with one another: membership stretches from Hawick to Inverness, and many folk are quite isolated – particularly in more rural areas. CWO and MWM have been able to hold meetings together.

There is a shortage of priests – there can be no doubt about that. We are constantly asked to pray for vocations, and rightly so, for the statistics make grim reading. I recently spoke with a friend who lives in a more remote part of Scotland. Her town has no resident priest, and she talked openly about the difficulties encountered because of this. A quick glance through the Catholic Directory shows how many priests are looking after two and even three parishes. Some communities are not able to attend Mass every Sunday simply because there are not enough priests. Isn't it unreasonable that many priests suffer from stress caused by overwork while at the same time the church does not seem to be able or willing to explore other types of ordained ministry? Are people to be deprived of the sacraments because there are not enough single, celibate men to administer them?

As a member of CWO, I am committed to supporting women's ordination. I continue to wear my badge and my purple ribbon. I continue to attend vigils, meetings and special events. There are many others like me, some of whom also feel that they personally may be called to ordained ministry. Unlike the men, we are not even given the opportunity to undergo a process of vocation discernment. We have never given up on the church. Many of us are active members of our parishes: serving as readers, coffee makers, musicians and in so many other valuable ministries. For our dedication we are told that we do not have the right even to discuss issues which we feel are important for us and for the church. I will continue to study, to pray and to protest. This is the waiting time. Perhaps the sequel to this chapter will bring the good news that my waiting is over.

13   *Inside out*

Ruth Harvey

The loom

I remember seeing my first loom in a dark cottage on the village street of Iona. I went there with my mum to ask Willie Coll, the weaver, if we could buy some of his tweed to make dresses. I remember the darkness and Uncle Willie Coll's wry smile as he showed us his tweeds. I also remember the vast loom with wires and threads and wools of many shades, and shuttles and shafts. It's an image I don't often recall. But when I think of the story of ministry in my life, of the many threads that make up the story, of the unfinished nature of this particular tweed, of the choices and chances that will determine the pattern, then I think of the loom.

Setting the loom

There are many threads that give shape to the story of ministry in my life. First there is the *thread of community*. This is a bold blue and green thread which dips and curves in a splendid pattern from the very beginning of my existence. At times it is a strong, secure, comforting thread. At other times it seems to be translucent, almost disappearing, submerged by the power and pattern of other threads. But of all the threads in my life I know that this one is the most sure, the rock on which the rest of my life stands.

Then there is the *thread of church* weaving its way through my life. Again I can identify this thread pulsing back to my beginnings. It has a red, orange, strident colour, and the line feels often thin, yet imperishable. Sometimes the colour is washed out and faded; almost dead. At other times the texture and colour and size give the impression that this thread dominates, has a grip, holds on tightly to the pattern. At these times this thread scares me and I feel overpowered. Often it is a beautiful, luscious orangy-red, gently weaving colour and compassion into the pattern.

The *thread of conviction* is the third thread that I would like to identify here. It has a yellow colour, and like the sun it can appear sometimes weak and clouded over, at other times on fire, alive. Like the other threads, the story of this thread in my life is a story of rich variety, with many textures, colours and subtle shades giving it its form.

A fourth thread is the *thread of people and relationships*. This is a multicoloured thread. The fuchsia and mushroom colours mix with deep purples and turquoise and speak of nourishment and warmth. The greys and blacks speak of times of desolation and loneliness. There are parts that are flamboyant and fluffy, full of rich experiences. There are parts that are tied into sharp knots, any further tugging only serving out more pain – these parts need tender care and much patient unknotting. This thread feels the most dynamic and diverse, the most hopeful and encouraging, because this is the thread from which I draw most energy and in which I invest most hope and faith.

Each thread has an undisclosed future. Together they weave a pattern that I am only beginning to understand. At times it seems like they go around in circles, doubling back on each other, repeating patterns that I had almost forgotten or had wanted to lay aside. I have a sense of belonging to these threads but no sense of control over their journey or over the bigger picture that they present. And of course I feel and scramble my way around the edges of my pattern of threads, where I encounter other intricate patterns of lives and life around me.

There are times when I can stand back a little and take a look at the pattern, watch how it is forming, give thanks for the glorious swishing patterns that are emerging, feel regret and embarrassment for some of the patches that are included. Dipping into the pattern of my life today, I can see some of the threads and their colour and texture, their form and size.

A swatch sample

Since May 1996 I have been working as Director of the Ecumenical Spirituality Project (ESP), a project that was established in 1989 and is an initiative of Churches Together in Britain and Ireland (formerly the Council of Churches for Britain and Ireland). The ESP was founded to enable and encourage dialogue between the many communities, projects, agencies and networks on the edges of the established church and the church as institution. Both the content of this work and the way in which it is carried out reflect my vision of ministry.

There is only one full-time worker for this project (a part-time administrator helps out). Because I know that I work best as part of a team, and that creativity flows most freely in collaboration with others, I try whenever possible to work on particular projects in small teams. A series of conversations (one-day workshops) exploring spirituality in an urban context was planned with a colleague. Workshops devised for use with small groups at Greenbelt were thought out with another colleague. A book that the ESP has commissioned is being edited by a team of five of us. In all of these mini-projects there is an unwritten understanding: that as soon as the process towards a book or a workshop becomes *only* another demand on time, *only* a burden, then it is reassessed. Hard work is part of the deal, but not hard work for its own sake.

The ESP runs on a shoestring budget. We don't have enough money to employ a second director. What we do have is a network of colleagues, people working in similar but discrete areas where interests overlap and skills are complementary. Finding ways to collaborate is not always easy – often I think it would be easier just to get on with it myself! But the rewards are always rich, and new ideas flourish in the process.

Ministry for me is about collaboration, hard work, sharing with people a vision but struggling together to listen to each other and to find an effective way forward, and about knowing when to say, 'Stop, this isn't working,' or 'Let's go on, we've got something here.' Ministry is about working alongside and resourcing people who are experts in their own field, whether it is urban spirituality, conflict resolution, youth work or publishing.

I have chosen so far not to be ordained to *the* Ministry of Word and Sacrament, believing what I have been encouraged to believe about ministry (no 'the') by the threads that weave their way through my journey: explore new patterns of ministry, do not be confined by ecclesiastical right ordering, search for the kind of ministry that Jesus would have you follow, look for the thread of the Holy Spirit and follow the colour and the texture where she leads.

The thread of community

The blues and greens of community begin with my family and my childhood where I was surrounded by clergy but didn't know that was what they were. The distinction between my father who wore a dog-collar on a Sunday and my mother who took me to nursery school was blurred when it came to the shared meal on a Thursday when the other members of the Gorbals Group arrived. Prayers happened in our living room as much as in the church. We grew up in inner-city Glasgow, on one of the most deprived housing estates in western Europe in the 60s. I didn't know that was where I was. I didn't know that I was living in an intentional community, ecumenical, committed to living alongside the poor.

At the age of five the focus shifted to Iona. There I learned that each day began with a service in the Abbey, followed by school, playing, food, homework, another service and a ceilidh or a concert if we were allowed to stay up. Worship was part of the package of daily life. I didn't know I was living on an island which some named 'the cradle of western Christianity'. I had no idea that my parents had chosen to opt in to shared food, shared money, shared homes. I didn't really understand why all these tourists kept coming to visit. I only knew that going to school with four other people was quite good fun, and waving goodbye to all my friends as they left each Saturday morning was difficult, and that going to the Abbey for services twice a day was normal.

That was my community experience as a child.

As an adult the hues become stronger and richer, and sometimes more strained as I began to have to make decisions and choices for myself. First I opted to join the community of the Student Christian Movement. As a member of the SCM I was an equal with other members in decision-making and in programme-setting. I was part of the collective. I took my turn in preparing food and washing up, in planning opening worship and closing prayers, in chairing the meetings and developing new techniques for creative listening. It was in this context that worship blossomed for me. I began to realise that I could have a part to play in shaping services. I could write poems that were prayers. I could explore the Bible and ask questions and begin discussions. I was accountable to a group, which meant that I had to take responsibility for what I said, so I was always challenged to think. We had no named leader or 'expert', but were each expected to 'minister' to the other.

This experience grew and deepened when I worked for a year with the World Student Christian Federation in Amsterdam. What I had experienced as a student in Scotland suddenly took on a whole new dimension when I was helping plan a workcamp in eastern Poland, or a seminar in Strasbourg, or a study visit to Hungary. How did the people of God share words and songs in worship when those people between them represented perhaps ten different languages and more cultures?

We found a way and I discovered a depth of sharing that is incomparable. Through sharing our understanding of key political and social issues of the time our horizons were blasted open. Through experiencing together orthodox liturgies in Slavonic and Lutheran masses in Finnish our faith was challenged and nourished.

It was with this background in ecumenical living in Amsterdam that I made the joint decision to offer myself as a new member to the Iona Community and as a candidate for the ministry to the Church of Scotland. From the perspective of a foreign country it felt right to shift my focus back home again. One year being courted in the international ecumenical community was long enough for me to realise that I was in danger of losing my rooted-ness. This joint decision was a conscious orientation of my life around two equally strong pulls. I had the strong sense that I could remain a member of and work in the Church of Scotland if I had membership of a community on the critical edge of that institution. I was also aware that my membership of the Iona Community would be strengthened if I was at the same time committed to my ecclesial community.

The church thread

I started at chapter one and read through to chapter eight, by which time I was falling asleep. It was my first night at Selection School, where my candidacy for the Church of Scotland ministry was being tested, and I wanted to remind myself of the first church, of the calling to ministry that those early apostles had felt, as recorded in Acts. The reading must have been inspirational because I was duly selected and began studying theology at New College, Edinburgh. Throughout my training at college and then as a probationary minister in Leith I was keen to carry on this exploration. How did what the church was teaching me to do and be relate to the calling of those earliest 'ministers'?

Studying theology opened up for me whole new avenues of liberation and contextual theology, ethics and the moral codes of society, church law and the ecclesiology of ministry. I was inspired by the many who came to our college from the south world, who talked of the need to study, to teach even, but then to return home to where the issues of faith, ethics and worship co-mingled on the margins of society. I wanted to do that too. And all the indications from my church, from my lecturers, from my advisers were that that was where sound ministry should be: on the margins, at the place of co-mingling.

I was faced with a challenge. How was I to live with the tension of the calling of the Spirit on the one hand and the calling of the church on the other? My experience was that while these new avenues of thought and theology were opening up, while I was being encouraged to explore collaborative ministry and new models of working together that would ensure the life of the church into the future, while I was encouraged to join a student community where we lived together and worked as an ecumenical team among the homeless in Edinburgh, while I was being convinced of the theology of the priesthood of all believers and of the absurdity of much religious pomp and regalia, while I was being inspired by the worker priest movement and being persuaded by the experiences of liberation theology, I was at the same time being told quite categorically that my first job had to be in a parish, where I might have to argue my way out of a large lonely manse, argue my way out of a dog-collar and robes, work hard to de-hierarchise my position as The Minister, take a stand if I wanted to re-form my job as a job-share.

Some of my best friends and many in my family are ordained clergy. They are struggling with some of the issues that I struggled with. And one day, who knows, I may also become ordained. But at that stage I knew two things in my gut: I was being called to develop a lay ministry that was true, as far as it could be, to the teaching that had influenced me through community and college, where all are ordained to do God's work, where there are no distinctions in pay or pension or pedigree, the only distinction being the gifts that we have been given uniquely by the Holy Spirit. I also knew that, as women were at last being ordained to the priesthood in the Church of England and then the Scottish Episcopal Church, there was a need for an exploration of what it would mean either to stop ordaining people to ministry as we know it so far or to devise new patterns of prayer and liturgy to reflect the many types of calling to ministry that God has ordained for us. I wanted to be part of that exploration. And I wanted to be part of it from a lay perspective.

My life at college was followed by a six-month gap which I grandly called my 'Ministry Orientation Project' (MOP) during which I explored other areas of ministry in community work and academic study. This gave me a breathing space, time to reflect on all that I had learned, time to make decisions about where I could go from there. I moved from there into a fifteen-month period as a full-time assistant minister in Leith. During this probationary period we had to attend seven conferences for probationary ministers. It was at the last of these that we were each asked to present our 'vision of ministry'. My time in Leith had been a healing one, working alongside a minister for whom I had great respect, in a parish where the local church did make a difference. Nevertheless I was by now convinced that for the time being I was not called to ordained ministry. Having to present my vision helped me focus on many of the issues I have outlined above. I left that conference feeling renewed, relieved and a little scared about where I would go from there. But I had been honest. I had 'come out' as a lay woman, and it felt good.

I am still part of the church. I still belong to the church and indeed work for an agency of the churches. This is where I belong, where I know the language and feel drawn to the wider, shared calling which is to make visible the Kingdom of God here on earth. So the orange and the red of the church thread in my life is still there, strong sometimes, sure, at other times whining and strident. Sometimes it fades and I feel a lesser person for its fading. Always I am moving towards a time when the blues and greens of community can mingle with the colours and shades of church, so making a richer pattern together.

The thread of conviction

There is a yogic exercise which encourages the practitioner to imagine that with each in-breath you breathe in light which begins at the top of the spine and travels downwards. With each out-breath that light is then sent to every corner of the body. As the meditation continues so the light continues to soak into the spine, coursing its way to each bodily extremity. In my varied attempts to pray, to communicate with God, to enhance my listening capacities and to be open to receive light from God, this exercise helps. The image of light filling my life is an image that gives me hope and courage – and yellow for me is the colour of hope and courage.

Where and when do I feel the conviction of faith that God, the Holy Spirit, Jesus is with me on my journey? What place does prayer have in my search for a calling to ministry?

This thread is vibrant when I am praying with others. Over the last two years a group of five of us have been meeting once a month, to eat together, to study the Bible and to pray. We choose themes for study that reflect our concerns and interests. Our prayers come out of these discussions and are made in the form of silence, songs, painting together, lighting candles. In the sharing of our concerns we listen hard to one another.

Over the years together we have developed a degree of trust and honesty which enhances this sharing. My vision of church is that groups of people can meet with joy and anticipation, share their concerns honestly with each other, share food, and offer these concerns, hopes and fears in the presence of each other to God. My vision of ministry is that we in the churches will recognise those who have the gift of enabling this process to happen and will encourage small, seemingly insignificant 'gatherings' like this to grow.

The thread of conviction is vibrant when I spend time alone, in contemplation. These are often dark times for me. It takes a while to be secure enough in my own company to let the light penetrate. So I avoid these times. But when I have them I realise the value of silence, of space, of quiet. When I read John of the Cross, study the words of Gerry Hughes, walk amongst the trees on my nearby hill, sit in front of my fire, the yellow thread pulses with energy and I feel strangely naked. My vision of church is that individuals can be freed to spend time alone with God and not feel they have to verify that freedom on a Sunday morning. My vision of ministry is that a climate of self-expression will be enabled to grow within the context of a rooted, communal ministry.

The thread of conviction is alive when my life connects with the story of Jesus. When I can identify with his anger in the temple. When I can identify with his wry words to the Pharisees. When I see others acting out his call for justice and can join in with that act. When I can imagine him sitting beside me on the train, on the bus, at my desk, during a workshop. When I recognise aspects of his character in my colleagues, my friends, UN peace-keepers, the Truth and Reconciliation Committee in South Africa. During these times, when I am able to recognise the presence of Christ, then the knowledge that I must keep on believing in him is strong. My vision of church is that we will recognise Christ in the most unlikely places and there be able to say, 'Ah, church!' My vision of ministry is that it will be a vehicle through which the Bible and other wise texts can come alive, drawing on the insights and experience of those with little or no formal training who nevertheless walk in Christ's path.

People weaving threads

There can be no comprehensive list of the people who are woven into the fabric of my life. There is no doubt, however, that it is those close to me who have shown me the way when the patterns in my life become confusing or complicated. Above all, it is those who have trusted me and urged me to believe in myself whose threads meander most strongly in the weaving.

There is a strong thread of ordained clergy in my family. My uncles, father, grandfather, great-grandfather and great-great-grandfather were or are all Church of Scotland ministers. It is to their credit that they watched me move close to their profession, then move away again, and never once pressurised me to 'join up'. It is also perhaps a reflection of their own broad understandings of ministry. Alongside this clergy line is a strong line of women in my family who have not kept silent, who have 'ministered' through hospitality, working alongside the poor, social work, mothering, advising and counselling. Perhaps more than the men, these women have shown me how God's ministry defies labels and right ordering. They have never pressurised me to become ordained.

At times this freedom was crippling – in my more insecure moments I wanted my parents to tell me what to do, to give me firm boundaries, to instruct me in my life decisions. The only firm instruction I could squeeze out of them was that I was to do what

I felt was best, and that they would uphold and support me in that decision. I remember once asking my parents why I had to be a Christian, just because they were. Why couldn't I be a Hindu or a Buddhist if I wanted to. They said that if I came home and told them I was a Christian *just* because they were, they would encourage me to go away and think again. And if I came home and told them I was a Hindu or a Buddhist and they could detect truth and integrity in that decision then they would support me. Infuriating! I was testing them and they wouldn't play my game!

Now I see the wisdom of their counsel, but at the tender age of fifteen I wanted more clarity and couldn't get it. This model of authority, of parenting, while by no means perfect has had and continues to have a huge influence on my life.

In a similar way friendships have been important places of growth for me. In the knots and painful breaking of some threads I have reluctantly been able to recognise growth points. I remember well a conversation with one woman who said she could never be my friend if I always agreed with what she said. I learned the hard way that I had to think for myself but that I had also to speak out and not be afraid to contradict or question those closest to me. In that learning process I became aware that friendship is not about being a 'yes-woman' but about plain speaking and unconditional love. I would hope that in a model of ministry based on friendship this kind of love and plain speaking could be at the core.

Weaving on: the bigger picture

It would be false to imply that these various threads weave happily and cleanly together to form a beautiful blanket that will wrap me up snugly in the depths of winter. False because it would deny the pain and the emptiness that is part of the picture. False because it would imply a completed object, dead, functional. False because it could easily become idealised. My vision for ministry is wrapped up in the many threads that I have described above. It is a vision which I hope will go on growing, as I add new threads and colours, and perhaps unpick some pieces to have a closer look at the components. I would like to end by identifying some hoped-for threads as the picture of ministry for the church of today and tomorrow unfolds.

Firstly, I would like to think that in ministry for the next millennium we could develop liturgies that respond to people's lives and experience. The ministry of 'Kairos in Soho' among gay and lesbian seekers who wish their relationships to be blessed by God and are developing liturgies to feed this need is one example of where this is happening. I would hope that in a similar way, for those people who live with one foot in the Christian faith and one foot in another world religion, where liturgies of the established churches mean little, new forms of worship could be devised with integrity to speak their language.

Secondly, I am encouraged by the groups of women who are meeting together to share their understanding of what it means to be women in leadership positions, lay and ordained, within the church. A small ecumenical group calling itself 'Lydia' has met twice now with this exploration in mind. This group and others like it will offer models for new forms of ministry for the future.

Thirdly, I have a hope that the gulf between those on the inside of the established churches and those on the edges, on the boundaries, or way beyond the edges, will be filled. This gulf, in my experience, is often bridged when folk speak honestly about their longings and doubts. The Greenbelt and Glastonbury Festivals could be places for this exploration to happen. Each attracts large numbers of people, many of them young, who are searching for something beyond the material, yearning for a deeper meaning in life. This yearning is a common thread which links devout Christians and new age travellers. My dream would be that those at each end of the spectrum can experience mutual nourishment without compromising belief or fearing the other.

These are only a few of the longed-for threads that I hope will be part of the continued weaving of the pattern of ministry into the future. As a woman, as a lay woman, I am both delighted and a little scared to identify myself within the pattern.

PROTEST FOR PEACE

Bernadette Meaden

Documenting the work of Christian peace activists, whose radicalism often places them on the fringes of the Church, this book will help their actions to be better recognised by their fellow Christians and by the wider community. It shatters the popular perception of Christians as conventional, respectable and passive.

In covering various different aspects of the peace movement, *Protest for Peace* explains the issues and recounts the personal experiences of some of those involved, including clergy and lay people who have served prison sentences as a result of direct non-violent action and are prepared to do so again. This alternative vision of what it means to be a Christian depicts a radical, compassionate faith that challenges the status quo, including the position of the churches on peace issues.

180pp. approx. · 1 01557 20 0 · £8.99 approx. · June 1999

THE PATTERN OF OUR DAYS

Liturgies and resources for worship from the Iona Community
Edited by Kathy Galloway

This inspiring anthology, reflecting the life and witness of the Iona Community, is intended to encourage creativity in worship.

Liturgies: Pilgrimage and journeys • Healing • Acts of witness and dissent • A sanctuary and a light. Resources: Beginnings and endings of worship • Short prayers • Prayers for forgiveness • Words of faith • Thanksgiving; Concern • Litanies and responses • Cursings and blessings • Reflections, Readings and meditations.

1996 ·192pp · 0947988 76 9 · £7.99

FOR GOD'S SAKE . . . UNITY
Maxwell Craig (Ed)

Many ordinary people yearn to pray and worship together in a way that reflects how they act together in their daily lives. This book gives voice to those longings and is an olive branch of hope in a Church currently torn along denominational lines. It is aimed at raising awareness of the need for unity among Christians and takes a look at progress to date, as well as at the long road still to be travelled.

Contributors include Kathy Galloway, Gerard W. Hughes, Jean Mayland, Martin Conway, John Fitzsimmons, Murdoch MacKenzie and Elizabeth Templeton.

1998 · 192pp ·1 901557 08 1 · £9.99

If you would like to receive a copy of our latest catalogue, please contact us at:

Wild Goose Publications
Unit 16, Six Harmony Row
Glasgow G51 3BA

Tel 0141 440 0985
Fax 0141 440 2338
e-mail: admin@wgp.iona.org.uk

The Iona Community

The Iona Community is an ecumenical Christian community, founded in 1938 by the late Lord MacLeod of Fuinary (the Revd George MacLeod DD) and committed to seeking new ways of living the Gospel in today's world. Gathered around the rebuilding of the ancient monastic buildings of Iona Abbey, but with its original inspiration in the poorest areas of Glasgow during the Depression, the Community has sought ever since the 'rebuilding of the common life', bringing together work and worship, prayer and politics, the sacred and the secular in ways that reflect its strongly incarnational theology.

The Community today is a movement of over 200 Members, around 1,500 Associate Members and about 700 Friends. The Members – women and men from many backgrounds and denominations, most in Britain, but some overseas – are committed to a rule of daily prayer and Bible reading, sharing and accounting for their use of time and money, regular meeting and action for justice and peace.

The Iona Community maintains three centres on Iona and Mull: Iona Abbey and the MacLeod Centre on Iona, and Camas Adventure Camp on the Ross of Mull. Its base is in Community House, Glasgow, where it also supports work with young people, the Wild Goose Resource and Worship Groups, a bimonthly magazine (Coracle) and a publishing house (Wild Goose Publications).

For further information on the Iona Community please contact:

The Iona Community
Pearce Institute,
840 Govan Road
Glasgow G51 3UU
T. 0141 445 4561; F. 0141 445 4295
e-mail: ionacomm@gla.iona.org.uk